A LIE IS A DEBT

A LIE IS A DEBT

A Psychological Novel
by June Stephenson, Ph.D.

Library of Congress Catalog Card No. 83-71777
ISBN 0-941138-02-X

Other Books by June Stephenson

The Administrator
Humanity's Search for the Meaning of Life
It's All Right to Get Old
Women's Roots

Diemer, Smith Publishing Co., Inc.
3377 Solano Avenue, Napa, CA 94558

*Dedicated to
My Daughters
and to Theirs*

Typesetting and production by Hillside Setting
Cover illustration by Jeri J. Johnston

Contents

Chapter 1

"Mother"

My daughter had been hurt. The sounds of Catherine's crying came through to me over the telephone, rasping on my nerve endings just as they did when she was a little girl. My instant impulse now was to help her, to "make it better."

"Mom," she sobbed from five hundred miles away, "Kevin just left me . . . I don't understand. We love each other." She was unable to tell me more when her crying got in the way. She wept, "I'll call you back," and hung up.

With the phone still in my hand I tried to hang on to her, not wanting her presence to fade while she was unhappy. The disconnection left me helpless to help her. I would not feel all right again until I knew she was all right.

It was easier to help both my girls when they were little. It was important to me that I or someone else were always available for them when they were hurt.

1

Because when I was little there was no one to run to, and I needed to offer what I had missed.

As a child when I ran home crying, for repairs to a skinned knee or elbow, I knew I was running to an empty house. There was no one home to cry to. My father was at work and, after I was eight years old, we no longer had babysitters. My mother had never been a part of our household because she had died when I was born.

When Catherine or Anne hurt themselves I could "make it better" with a band-aid or a kiss. Or I could easily distract them with a pretty flower, or a picture book. Even when Catherine was seriously injured, knocked down to the concrete and suffering a brain concussion, I could still comfort her as we sped to the hospital. But as she and Anne grew older I began to see that the hurts that went deeper than skin and bone were the ones that were harder to make better. And because I couldn't help as easily, I suffered more for them when their feelings were hurt. There were no band-aids for the hurts of the heart.

My own growing up and talks with my father persuaded me that people had to work out their personal problems for themselves.

"That way you'll be strong," my father would say when the kids at school made fun of my clothes because there was no mother in our house to iron or mend. "Put your mind to something else. Find something to do. Don't dwell on unhappiness." It wasn't that he was insensitive. He was the only parent my brother and I had, and he wanted us to learn to depend on ourselves.

He taught me that crying too long about things the other kids said did no good. And of course I believed he was right because he was my father and because I loved him. Then, when I became a parent I attempted to follow my father's kind of parenting, though at times it seemed too stern. I wanted to raise Catherine and Anne in ways that were more sympathetic instead of in ways that taught them "to take it."

I would have liked my husband to feel as I did, but his attitude was much like my father's. I had not thought so when my husband and I first met. I believed I had seen more kindness, maybe because that was what I was looking for. One of the first things that attracted me to Bob was his criticism of the South's treatment of Blacks long before there was a Civil Rights Movement. At that time I thought he cared about people who were unfortunate. Much later I saw that his feelings were not so much sympathy for the Blacks as scorn for southern Whites. But it takes a long time to get to know another person's inner workings, even in marriage.

At the beginning of World War II, after almost three years of dating, making love, breaking up and making up again, we were married. The night before Bob had to appear at the Selective Service he asked me, almost as a doomed man, "If I'm classified I-A will you marry me?"

He knew I would.

Though the years before our marriage were stormy, after our marriage our life together was smoother. We had many problems, but not with each other. Living together in small towns on the outskirts of army camps across the country, we learned to live with ration stamps, rent controls, cramped living quarters, constant new acquaintances, and very little money. We were as two people thrown into a new river who didn't know the current, the depth, or the unexpected obstacles. In our new life there were no familiar landmarks and no friendly faces. We had only each other and we learned to navigate together.

We survived all those difficulties, even the army's shifting Bob from the east coast to the west coast for no apparent reason. I could pack up all our things in a few hours and be on the Overland Express train shortly after I saw Bob off on his troop train. Then I'd scurry around the new town nearest to the army camp where he was stationed. I would "scout the territory," as Bob would say. The want ads were not always the best source for finding a place to live. Rentals were so scarce landlords didn't need to advertise.

I'd usually find a room to rent in someone's house and that would be my base of operation. Then there was the anxiety of not knowing how long it would be before a corporal as Bob was, could be allowed to live off the base, if at all. And there was the anxiety too of wondering how soon I could get a job.

Employers were reluctant to hire army wives because we were not permanent residents. But fortunately because it was wartime, there was a labor shortage and I always managed to find some sort of secretarial work whether it was in Nebraska, or Georgia, or Vermont.

Bob came into town from camp when he could get away. Some of his commanding officers allowed their men to live off base, some would let their men go into town in the evening but required them to return to the base before midnight, and some would permit only weekend passes unless the company was restricted to the base because of military maneuvers, or because someone had not had a clean foot locker during inspection.

Life together was tenuous and precious.

When the war ended Bob was on Okinawa about to be part of the landing forces going in to attack Japan. I cried with the relief that he had not been killed.

I met his returning troop ship one early Sunday morning, caught a glimpse of him on deck and then watched him march down the ramp, a heavy pack on his back. Overseas he had been promoted to sargeant and he was leading his platoon to busses waiting to take them to evacuation centers for discharge from the army.

He spotted me in the crowd of wives and children, changed his direction and ran toward me, his platoon automatically following him. We embraced, holding on to each other, while his platoon broke rank and cheered their sargeant.

We picked up our life where we had left off before the war. Bob finished his Master's degree in Business Administration and after two more years, his Ph.D. in economics. He took a job with a new company called I.B.M. and as I.B.M. prospered, so did we. Bob was promoted and transferred to Chicago, then to Los Angeles, New York, and New Orleans. Each time he was given new responsibilities and with each promotion he was away from home longer hours.

During those first years after the war ended I worked as a secretary to help Bob through his graduate degrees. Then as he was promoted and transferred I quit jobs and found others even after our two daughters were born. Though Bob's salary was adequate to support us, his long hours and my need to feel part of the world outside of small children kept me working.

It was a nice coincidence that after

the babies were born we could stop moving from city to city because I.B.M. promoted Bob to the assistant west coast manager position in San Francisco. Our lives began to settle down. For ten years we had moved, first with the army and then with I.B.M. Now for the first time we had a real sense of belonging to a community when we bought a house in Burlingame south of San Francisco.

I joined the University Women's Club, later the girls joined the Brownies, and years later Bob became president of the girls' elementary school Parent Teachers Association.

"It's to help the bond issue," he explained, "but it will also help the company."

"What do you mean? How can being president of the P.T.A. help I.B.M.?"

"Well of course I'm doing it for the school bonds, but it will also be good for the company."

"Bob, I don't understand. What does being P.T.A. president have to do with I.B.M.?" I asked again.

"A great deal! The company wants its men to get involved in the community, to keep up a good company image."

8

"Bob, you astound me! What's the connection..."

"Can't you see? P.T.A. is one small step. Maybe I'll run for the school board. Show my interest in this town. Get to know people, the movers, the decision-makers, prove to the company, you know, leadership and all that." He lit his pipe. "Did you know that Jenny Birch on the P.T.A. Executive Council is also on the City Council?"

"No. I didn't." And I hadn't really cared. Not then. Years later Jenny Birch was going to play a bigger part in my life, but right then she was only a name. I didn't see any connection between Bob's ambition and Jenny. I felt let down. I had thought Bob's interest in the P.T.A. was his interest in his children. It was disturbing to suspect that he was using the P.T.A., and indirectly his children, for his personal promotion.

From that time on I began to understand that anything was justifiable if it were for the company. Extra hours away from home. Buying drinks late into the night for company prospects. Catered dinners in our home for city council members, county supervisors, planning commission members, joining the Burlingame Country Club and playing golf every Sunday, "to get to know the right people." I didn't know whether the company was consuming Bob or if he drew his life's blood from the company. Whatever the arrangement, it scared me. So much so that when the promotion from assistant manager to manager was imminent, I begged Bob not to take it.

"You're making a lot of money now, and what good is it? We're losing each other."

I could see that my words irritated him as they always did whenever I mentioned my fear of our drifting away from each other, but I continued anyway. "You're away from home so much now. If you take that promotion you'll never be home. The girls will be in junior high school next year. A few more years and they'll be gone. Someday you may wish..."

"Dammit, Lisa, if the promotion is offered, I can't refuse. Too many people under me are counting on me to take that job. It's been in the works for years." He chewed on the stem of his pipe.

"But Bob, your job is already hurting

us. We've been losing each other. With a new promotion..."

"It's not the job that's hurting us, Lisa." He stopped chewing and pointed the stem of the pipe at me. "It's you! You don't help! You're fighting me when I have to work late. Or, like now, this promotion. Any other wife would be overjoyed, supportive. I'm out there all alone." His pipe went back in his mouth, hanging in the corner, unlit.

"Alone! *You're* alone! Where do you think I am! It's the kids and me...alone. When are you here?"

"Lisa, I'm doing all I can. You know the pressures on me. Christ sake, you think I want to work like a slave? Don't put your pressures on me." He pointed his pipe at me again. "Everything I do is for you and the girls."

He could make me feel guilty.

Even so, I tried one more time. The night before Bob accepted the promotion I begged him again to turn it down, but my efforts were wasted.

As West Coast Manager Bob worked even longer hours and he often stayed overnight in San Francisco. Rumors of affairs with other women reached me, but I refused to believe them until one day when I was taking his suits to the dry cleaners.

I had forgotten to empty his pockets. The lady at the counter dumped small change, matches, and an open package of Trojan condoms on the counter.

I had used a diaphragm for the last twelve years.

The clerk smiled sheepishly. I stared at the things on the counter, not moving.

She gathered everything together and pushed the pile toward me. I turned and walked out.

When I got up enough courage to talk to Bob about it he became angry. "God dammit, Lisa, why do you have to be so suspicious. I thought we might try condoms for a change. You're always complaining about having to get out of bed for your diaphragm. Thought we might have more sex if we had rubbers handy. Wrecked the first one pulling it out of the package. Guess I'm not," he laughed and put his arm around me, "as adept as I used to be."

He laughed again and withdrew his arm. "Remember when we were going together how I could open those up without breaking my stride, remember...out on the beach?''

That's what he could do. Pull my mind away from disaster and soothe me with old, sweet memories. I knew he was lying about the Trojans but I wanted to believe his lie.

After that promotion the two or three before-dinner martinis increased to five or six. "That commute traffic is getting thicker," he'd explain. "Enough to drive a man to drink." His good humor carried him through the first few martinis.

"Hold dinner, honey," he'd urge, "the kids are watching T.V. They can wait." Then later he'd bring up some subject to attack. One time it was about the company's best customer.

"Let me tell you about Swanson. Cut his last order after we processed it. Son-of-a-bitch shafts me every time. Tries to make me look bad."

"Not intentionally, I'm sure," I tried to subdue his rising anger.

"He's not smart enough to outwit me. I've got his number. Next time...Ha..." he laughed, "I'll lock him into a contract so tight he can't wiggle out."

"Bob, I need to talk to you about Anne," I started.

"I send in my regional reports, best

13

in five years. Swanson cancels and New York wants revisions...."

"Bob, I'm sorry about Swanson, but..."

"Son-of-a-bitch. Next time he wants a rush order he can just..." he mumbled something and poured his sixth martini. I took the pork roast out of the oven.

"Will you carve this?" I asked. I handed him the carving knife and fork and as he carved the roast I put the salad and vegetables on the table, called Anne and Catherine, and we all sat down to hear Bob tell us about the underhanded methods some customers use to discredit the man at the top.

"If you don't enjoy your job," I suggested as I often did, "why don't you...?"

"Get out of it? I can't get out of it now." He slowly placed a portion of meat on each of our plates while we waited for his usual reasons. "Maybe ten years from now I can quit...after I get the kids through college."

"The girls can get through college, somehow, if they want to. You don't have to keep a job that makes you miserable."

"Look, Lisa. Quit giving me your simplistic solutions. I can't quit now and you know it. The mortgage on this house would drown us if I had any other job." He dominated me with his narrowed eyes and I said no more. We all ate in silence. The discussion I'd wanted to have with him about Anne would have to wait. Or else I'd just resolve it myself as I usually did those days. Making all the decisions in the marriage left me feeling lonesome. I'd lost my partner of the earlier years.

Often I wanted to talk to him about our girls but he was either away from home or immersed in some company detail more important than our family problem. He would dismiss my attempt to interest him in the girls' little squabbles with demands that I quit babying them so they could grow up. I'd seen this attitude about Anne and Catherine developing when Catherine was in the fourth grade.

The school district doctor had advised that we move her to another school because of the persistent tormenting by three or four children in the classroom.

"Hard knocks are the stuff of life, Lisa," Bob told me then. Possibly that strong determination developed when he had to stand up to harassment when he was little, the only American boy in a private school in England. Then, later, after his parents moved back to the United States, he had to endure the ridicule of his classmates. His English accent made him the target of school jokes. But he had learned to take it. He had learned to be strong in the face of teasing. So he insisted that Catherine not be withdrawn from a hurtful predicament.

"If you move her out of that situation," he warned me, "she'll never be able to meet difficult situations in the future. She needs to face up to it with chin up." So I retreated from my impulse to "over-protect" her, as he described it. It was a familiar position for me. I could understand his reasoning, but I sympathized with Catherine every night when she cried and begged me to get her "away from those kids."

Many years later when Catherine was a skinny freshman in Burlingame High School and grew in height taller than any other students in the school including all the basketball players, all six feet of my daughter with her eye glasses and bands on her teeth was miserable.

"I'm a freak," she cried. "I walk down the hall and I see the tops of everybody's heads. No matter how well I do in school, or how good I am in sports, I'm a

16

freak!" And for her age she was.

How I wanted to put my arms around her and cry with her. No amount of telling her how beautiful she was going to be, helped ease the daily torment. Students, teachers, and for that matter almost anyone who talked with her referred to her as a "tall string bean," or they invariably asked, "How's the weather up there?" wounding her where she was already suffering.

When I agonized over Catherine's misery, trying to discuss it with Bob, he would dismiss it with, "She'll survive." And of course she did. In her senior year, with full figure, contact lenses, and straight teeth, the football team chose her as their Homecoming Queen.

From then on she had a relatively easy time of it. She appeared unscarred by either the strain of having been a "freak," or by having a distant relationship with her father. Off to college she began dating, and then falling in love for a time with one young man and then later with another. It was in her last year of law school that she met Kevin, the young man who had just left her.

He was for Catherine what other men had not been. His gracious manners appealed to her. She had always admired her father's style, though she had not always admired her father. Was it possible she saw a younger reflection of the father whose love she may have doubted? Possibly. In any case, Catherine had found what she had been looking for and she invested herself one hundred percent.

In her other love affairs I had seen a transitory casualness on her part. But when I saw Kevin and Catherine together, I felt they were making an investment in the future. I saw an attitude of permanence. I remembered that they had talked of setting up a law practice together. What of that now? But more to the point what of the shock of his leaving her? Always before she had been the one to leave an affair. How could she help herself over this unexpected jolt? How could I help her. How could I make it better?

How had we as parents taught her to survive difficulties like this? Would the lessons of her childhood help her now? Would her father's constant advice of "chin up," do any good? What of the image of her father in those last years before our divorce, blurry eyed and slurring his words? Was that a picture of a man who could take it "chin up?"

And what image did I present for her? I remembered how carefully I hid my own misery all the years our marriage was disintegrating. How carefully I had reserved my tears for the private moments when no one would know I was so weak that I cried with the shame of losing a beloved husband to mistresses, his job, and to alcohol.

"We know, Mom, about Dad's drinking," Anne said when I moved the three of us out of the house on that first step toward divorce. With a pretended calm, I picked Catherine and Anne up from Burlingame High School and explained that we would not be living in our beautiful home anymore. We were going to be living in an apartment I had moved us into while they were in school. I told them I was not going to live with Daddy anymore because of his drinking. I did not tell them of the other reasons.

"Dad is so stupid," Catherine cried then. "Why doesn't he just quit drinking?"

"Why does he drink all the time?" Anne asked. I hadn't known they had seen so much. I thought of the many nights I had actually lied to them, covering up for their father while we waited supper for him.

"We used to hear you arguing about Dad's drinking," Catherine confessed. I was surprised. My secret had not been a secret after all.

"One time we heard Daddy...well, it sounded like he hit you," Anne added. "We were scared."

I thought I had been so careful to insure that no one would know that I had been hurt either emotionally or physically. Especially I wanted my children to know that their mother was strong. I had always believed parents should be examples of courage. I did not want to be guilty of weakness. Yet from the upstairs landing of our home our girls had heard that I had been hurt physically and emotionally by their father. I had failed to keep my agony to myself. I felt ashamed and guilty.

But many years later I wondered what kind of contradictory messages both Bob and I had given to our girls. The image we presented to the public was of a serene marriage, but the image at home, I had learned, was quite different.

"You were the model of the happy, successful couple," people told me when I started our divorce. "We were shocked." The deception at least outside our home had been successful. But as for our children, they must have seen us as two sets of people, the public couple and the at-home couple. We had not been teaching them "to be strong." By example we had been teaching them to pretend they were strong. What, then, was strength? Where did it come from?

Even in the worst crisis of my life I had called upon my strength to help me cry alone, to pretend all was well. I seemed to be instructing our children as I moved in a daze through the early months of breaking up our family, "This is the way one does it. This is the way one ends a twenty-five-year marriage. This is the way you are to finish your last years in high school. You must pretend that you are not near to crying when you think about your parents' divorce. Think about something else. Don't dwell on un-happiness. This is the way we carry our heads up. Everyone in this community has a reason why I left a man they all admire. But they are wrong and we are above the rumors. We do not offer expla-nations., And we cry in private. Time will pass and the pain will lessen, but what we never do is break down in public and show our wounds."

And where, I wondered, had I acquired such fortitude? Had I learned that, too, from my dignified Swedish-born father who had lived for a quarter of a century in his own silent hell, one that I didn't know about until the Christmas Eve when I was twenty-five years old.

He told me about it when we were alone, waiting for Bob to return from a shopping errand my father had asked Bob to make. I had put the last few ornaments on the small Christmas tree and I was happy with the kind of expectancy of someone waiting for an unknown gift, when my father asked me, "Do you know that your mother is alive?"

I turned from the Christmas tree to look at him, unbelieving. My mother could not be alive because she had died when I was born. That's what I had been told when I was very small and that was what I had always known.

"When you were born..." my father began. He was quite nervous. He sat down on the large velour overstuffed chair, clasped his hands and concentrated on them. "Your mother was very sick." He spoke as though he had memorized what he had to say and was determined to go through with it. "There were no medicines then like there are now," he said and he paused.

"She got better." He paused again, deep in reflection. "Her body got better ... but something happened ... to her mind."

I didn't move. I waited. I felt I was somewhere else.

"It was melancholia," he continued. "That was what the doctor told me. She was ... she was supposed to get better ... They said many women get depressed after childbirth, but that ... it would pass. I waited. Weeks went by and then months.

"Some days," he spoke deliberately, slowly. "Some days she would be fine. I would think she was all well. We would be very happy together." He almost smiled. His thoughts had gone off into better days. "Then, at other times, I'd come home from work and realize she had been sitting and staring in the same chair for hours. And ... and you and Alec had not been fed and you were screaming ... you were both ... soiled. It was dangerous for you." He was quiet for a long time. I stood stunned, mute. "I thought maybe...you...both of you might die." He paused again, his eyes deep in his memories.

"I had to tell the neighbors," he said, embarrassed, lowering his head. "They started to help. We all thought they would help just until she got better. But ...she got worse." He stopped again.

I still had not moved. I knew what he was telling me was true, yet his speaking seemed unreal. Something was not penetrating my mind.

"Then," he said, coming out of another memory, "when you were seven months old they came to take her away to the state institution. I had to sign the papers."

There were tears about to fall from his eyes, but he mastered them, taking his eyes off his hands and looking at me. "And as far as I know," he forced himself to continue, "she is still alive. I don't know where she is. I heard," he said, "that they moved her several times. Your aunt told me that. She, too, has lost track of her."

"I have not gone to see her for fifteen years." He looked at his hands again and refolded them. "When I went to see her," he said, "she never knew me. It was too much for me. It did no one any good, not her, not me, to go to see her."

He swallowed. A tear dropped onto his hand. He smeared the tear away with his other hand and looked at me as a criminal looks at his confessor.

Finally I was able to move and to speak. "You have carried this secret all these years!" I went to him and sat on his lap as I did when I was small. Then he let fall all his tears and they ran down his cheeks, onto his vest and his hands and we both cried together. I held on to him, hugging him, our tears mixing on our faces. My heart hurt for a man who had kept that heavy secret for so long. What an example of bravery and courage he was for me!

"How could you keep such a secret?" I asked when I had stopped crying.

"I put it out of my mind," he said. "I didn't think about it. I put my mind on my work, grew flowers, thought about my children. I would not let myself dwell on unhappiness." He shook his head negatively as though not to let the thoughts in, even now.

"I did not want you or Alec to know this," he explained. "You, Lisa, were always so sensitive. I thought you might worry about it. I didn't think there was any reason you should ever know. It was hard for me to know. Things were difficult enough for both you and Alec, not having a mother."

"So you carried it all by yourself," I said in admiration. Then I wondered, if we had survived so well all those years without knowing, why was he telling me now?

He anticipated my question.

"There are people who know about this and they know you. You may never see any of these people, but on the other hand, one never knows. Someday someone might tell you about your mother.

"I made up my mind to tell you and Alec when...I met a lady...I'll tell you about her. I knew her parents. We belonged to the same Swedish social club. They're my age. They had adopted this lady when she was a baby and they never told her she was adopted. They always pretended that they were her real parents and she assumed they were. I knew they weren't. Other people knew too, but the parents asked all their friends not to tell her. Well, last year both the parents were killed in a car accident, and their will mentioned their adopted daughter. On top of losing her parents, she was very upset to learn that she was not their real daughter and they were not her real mother and father.

"She said what hurt her the most was that a stranger told her — the lawyer. She didn't believe him, because she said her mother and father would have told her if it had been true. He had to bring out all the papers to convince her. She cried when she told me. She felt betrayed.

"I would not want you to go through that. I don't want to take the chance that someone else might tell you."

Even though I was still in a strange, stupefied state, I appreciated what he had just told me. I was even thinking of the new possibility of having a mother for the first time.

"Could I find her?" I asked, wiping my own tears away.

"No. Please don't try to find her. There is no good in it. Trust that she was seen by the best doctors, that there was nothing that could be done. It was something I had to convince myself of and I believe it. There is nothing but more sadness for you and for me if you try to find her. As far as I know she is still alive, but I'm not sure of that."

How could I not agree with his wish? Why should my desire, my curiosity even, bring him more heartache. Hadn't he had enough! I agreed I would not look for her.

All those years my father had been putting Alec and me first, considering what was best for his children. He had never said how it must have torn him apart to put his wife in what was then called an insane asylum, or what it was like to live a single life raising two babies to adulthood. Hadn't he hoped for her return? Hadn't he looked at us and thought of her?

I remembered when people asked him why he didn't remarry, he would say he had loved only one woman and would never marry again. Now, though, I had more understanding.

"Your mother's sisters came to take you away," he said, smiling slightly now that the worst was told. "They would raise you, they said. They told me a man can't raise two children by himself." He smiled again, this time with pride. "I thanked them and told them to go back home. If I needed their help I would call for them.

"You children," he said, "were all

28

that I had left, and I wasn't going to give you away. You have been the joy of my life!" With that we both cried again and smiled at each other through our tears.

"I'm glad you didn't give us away," I said, hugging him again. I admired him for his inner strength that night more than I had ever admired any other human being — and he was my father!

Now, about thirty years later, as I waited for Catherine to phone me back, those recollections appeared and I began to wonder about courage. What good had it done my father? What had it cost him? Hadn't he felt guilty, protecting that lie from his children for twenty-five years? I had sympathized with his motives and I loved and admired him, but now these thirty years later I looked at it differently. In trading honesty for a kind of deceit, hadn't he put himself in debt? And at what cost to himself? At least when Alec and I were no longer little, why couldn't he have shared some of his pain?

Why couldn't I have shared mine?

What good had courage done me? When my marriage was crumbling I had kept up a phoney front. How I had admired my own strength! Yet what purpose did that serve? And Bob? In his early years had he really learned "to take it?" Or did he use alcohol to block the haunting possibility that he couldn't take it?

On the eve of this phone call from Catherine I began to see that the emotional roots we had given her were strong — too strong. In great crisis neither Catherine's father, nor I, nor any of her grandparents had cried for help. We had all believed that our suffering in silence was virtuous. But I was beginning to doubt all that.

We had been courageous.

We had met the near devastation of our lives in our own individual private and lonely separate hells.

Sitting and waiting for the telephone to ring, I thought of all those years wasted in bravery. I tried to picture things as they might have been. I imagined my father telling us as children what had happened to our mother. He had given us other responsibilities beyond our years and we had proved ourselves. Why not this? We might even have lightened his years without damage to ourselves.

Then I imagined Bob telling me of his secret fears, whatever they were. I saw myself reassuring him that he would still be admired even if he let his weakness show. I saw myself with Catherine and Anne, discussing their father's drinking and the possible alternatives for all of us, instead of all that cover-up.

What I saw in those illusions cut through the years of pretending and I wondered why it had taken me so long. It was something about Catherine's phone call. Something like the innocence of a small child had broken through her years of training "to take it on the chin" and had cried out for help. And the clarity of this innocence seemed to point the way for me.

I might not know what I would do, but I knew what I would not do. I would not tell her that heartbreak happens to all of us sometimes in our lives. I would not tell her how lucky she was that she and Kevin hadn't gotten married. I would not tell her that someone as beautiful and talented as she was would be back "in the swing" before long, or that hard knocks would make her strong, or that time would pass.

I would not tell her to go about her day as though everything were the same as it was yesterday. I would not tell her all the things that people say to others in distress to gain time — to stall.

The phone rang.

"Mom, I'm sorry I cried...."

"Whatever you do, Catherine," I said, "don't apologize for your tears. They're natural, and right now they're the best things you can do for yourself."

She was silent. I believed she was trying not to cry. "Mom...I'm so miserable...." Again, she gave in to her sobs. "I don't know what happened. He just said it would never work...and he left...."

Because of the gulps of sobs I could hardly understand her.

"Catherine, would you like me to fly down? I can take a few days off work..." I hadn't known I was going to say that, but when the words came out they were right. A relief!

"Could you? But Mom, I don't want to be a baby. If you come down, I guess it would mean I'm a baby."

"Who cares if you're a baby? Some of us at twenty-five, or forty-five, or any age sometimes are babies. We need help. We need to ask for help. I don't think it's such a great thing anymore to be the Rock of Gibraltar when your world is coming apart. If needing help means you're a baby — well, then, be a baby."

I could hear her crying again.

"I'll fix things at work tomorrow, day after tomorrow I'll catch a plane. Spend a few days with you. Okay?"

"Mom, thank you," she cried. "I'm sorry, I can't stop crying...."

"It's all right to cry," I said. "It's stupid not to. I'll see you soon honey. I'll try... I'll try to make it better."

"Thanks, Mom," she said, some of the tension going out of her voice.

Chapter 2

"Father"

I was unprepared for the hostility in Catherine's voice. Her few phone calls and letters were the only link between us after Lisa and I were divorced, and Catherine and I spoke only bland pleasantries, nothing serious. But this time it was different.

Usually she phoned to say she'd be in town visiting her mother and would ask me when it would be convenient for us to get together. We'd meet at a restaurant because Betty refused to see her, and this arrangement was easier on all of us.

When she phoned at two o'clock on that Saturday afternoon I was kind of hazy. I wasn't sure if I had phoned her first and she was phoning me back. I heard the phone ring six or seven times before I realized Betty wasn't going to answer it. I guess she had told me she was going out. I couldn't remember. So I let it ring a few more times while I freshened my drink. It was a pleasant surprise when I heard it was Catherine.

"Dad," she asked, "are you there?"

I guess I hadn't said hello. "Yeah... Oh... Catherine," I said, "it's you. Where are you, honey. You in town?"

"No. I'm in Hollywood."

"Well... why're you calling?" That didn't sound the way I had meant it. "I mean..."

"Dad... could you talk with me. Are you able to talk?"

"What do you mean? Sure I'm able to talk. You mean, is Betty here? No... I don't think she's here."

"No. That's not what I mean." I hadn't yet detected anything different in her voice. When I drank from my glass the ice cubes slid down and clinked on my teeth.

"You have a drink there?" Her voice changed. It wasn't friendly anymore.

"Yes. Noisy isn't it?" I laughed.

"Maybe I'll call you back." She sounded downright cold.

"Why call back? You're on the phone now. What's up, honey?"

"There's no use talking to you when you're drinking."

"Just because I have a drink beside me doesn't affect my ears," I laughed.

There was a long silence on the phone. I wondered if maybe she had hung up. I took another swallow, this time slower, so that the ice cubes would stay at the bottom of the glass.

"Cathy, you there?"

"Yes," she answered. I had to strain to hear her voice. "I'm here. But..." I thought she was going to say she'd changed her mind again and would call me back, but then she started in on me and I will never forget how surprised I was that she could attack me like that.

This was my little girl...my little girl all grown up, my own daughter turning on me. I couldn't get hold of any words to say because I was that unprepared.

"Wouldn't it be nice if I could call you up and find you sober. But that won't happen much now that you're retired. What else do you have to do besides drink!"

"Catherine...wait a minute...."

"Retired," she repeated. "I think you retired long ago. From being my father, I mean."

"What...what are you talking about? Catherine is that you?"

"Yes. This is Catherine. Only it's a different Catherine." Then I heard her voice change again, this time from anger. I even thought that she might be crying. "I wanted to talk to you...about something, about how you and I got along when I was growing up...or didn't get along, or something...because...because Kevin left me...." Then I did hear crying. "And all day today I've been trying to look at myself...to see what's wrong."

I know that she said a lot more than that but I was trying to figure out who Kevin was. I interrupted her. "Kevin?" I asked, "he's the young man you brought home with you at Thanksgiving?"

"Yes," she said, and then in her bored and impatient voice she asked, "you don't remember him? It was only a few months ago."

Well I couldn't be expected to remember them all by name. Seems each Thanksgiving there was a new one. This must have been the one who wore the vest. I thought at the time it was unusual for a young man to be wearing a three-piece suit. It was more like the old days. Kind of reminded me of myself when I got dressed up to take Catherine's mother out dancing when we were going together before the war. That boy...what was his name...Kevin, was it? Come to think of it, he had blonde hair and was built something like me. I guess a good physique is a plus for any man. Sure brings the girls on. My body did all right by me. I remember how Lisa used to run her hands over my chest. God, what love nights we had!

"Dad, you're not even listening."

"Sure I am," I said. "You said Kenneth left you. Well, he'll be back, honey...."

"It's not Kenneth, it's Kevin, and no, he's not coming back. Dad you make me so mad. I wanted to call you and talk to you because...because I need to and, and it's only two o'clock...."

"What's two o'clock got to do with anything? What's the time got to do with Kenneth? And how could he leave you?"

"It's not Kenneth," she practically yelled at me, "it's Kevin. And I should be able to talk to you at two o'clock because I can't talk to you at four or six because by four you're getting drunk and by six o'clock it's too late. Usually it's been okay to call you at this time. But now I can hear you're already where you used to be at four o'clock. So forget it."

She hung up.

I looked at the dead telephone in my hand and it made me angry. I wanted to use it like a hammer on the kitchen table. I wanted to smash something. Instead I slammed the phone down and fumbled in the telephone drawer for Catherine's number.

"This is your father," I emphasized. "I do not appreciate what you just said about my drinking." I expected her to say she was sorry. Then I would have told her that I didn't appreciate what she said about, what was it, about retiring as a father.

She didn't say anything.

"Catherine? You there?"

"Yes. I'm here," she answered.

"I want you to know," I told her firmly, "I am not drunk."

"I know Dad," she said with exaggerated patience. "You are never drunk."

Now she was getting it straight.

"It's just that after the sun starts going down you slur your words, you get unsteady on your feet, your eyes get glassy, you don't hear what people say, you repeat yourself over and over, but you're not drunk."

I had never heard her talk that way before. Then she started in again. "But in the morning you're your usual gentle-manly self, all polished and...and quick with your wit...and you never remember what you said the night before...you never know how you looked."

What was she talking about?

I think I must have hung up on the phone because I don't remember what I said and I don't remember if I called her back one more time. But I know it was on my mind the next morning when I woke up.

Betty was still in bed when I went into the kitchen and looked at the clock. It was close to noon. On Sundays that would be about the time for her to get up so I knew I should call Catherine right away. Anything having to do with my old life, like talking to my kids, upset Betty and then she'd be irritated about every little thing for days. To keep peace be-tween Betty and me I just ignored my old life. Just as well she didn't hear this con-versation.

At first when Catherine answered the phone she was reticent. I let her know I didn't like what she said yesterday and I expected her to apologize.

"I have no intention of apologizing," she said. "I call up because I need help in

41

trying to understand myself and even at two in the afternoon you're too drunk to listen to me. I can't remember when I had a father I could talk to. I don't know why I tried yesterday. I think I must have been desperate and...I wanted to believe..."

"Honey," I said, "you sure know how to hurt a guy. I'll let that stuff about being drunk go by for now, but not having a father to talk to...why I can remember lots of times."

"You can? Please tell me about them because I can't remember," she said.

"Well..." I had been thinking about this, so I was ready. "I can remember when you were in...was it the fourth grade? How you would come to me and cry and tell me how those kids used to go by your desk and knock your books and papers on the floor. Remember that?"

"Yes. I'll always remember that."

"Remember how you used to cry and tell me how they threw things at you and when the teacher was out of the room?"

"Yes, and I remember what you told me to do, to learn how to act like it didn't bother me, to take it on the chin and all those things. But Dad, that's not exactly what I'm talking about, though in a way

42

it is. I'm talking about...well there were so many times I wanted you to help me, but I couldn't go to you. I couldn't...I couldn't even ask you...." I heard her crying. That surprised me.

I knew she was upset about her boy-friend leaving, but I didn't think she was crying about that now.

"Cathy. Don't cry, honey. What is it you want me to do?"

"I know it sounds silly, Dad, and we've never had any good talks and now ...I hope it isn't too late, but I want us to do something we've never done be-fore...."

"Yes?"

"I'm wanting you to go back in your memory because..." and then she broke into crying again, "I...I think it's im-portant!"

"Sure, honey. What is it you want to remember? Fire away!"

"Well," she said, trying to get her voice in control, "when I was little I wanted you to...to hold me. Does that sound like so much? I don't remember you ever picked me up and...and held me."

I thought about what she said. Surely when she was little I must have held her

43

on my lap. It seems I remember doing that. She must not be remembering things right. She's upset. "I held you, Cathy, I know that. But why are you worrying about something like that now? You're not a baby. You're a woman now. You're talking about...more than twenty years ago!"

"I know," she said. "I'm talking about," and her words flooded out. I don't think I ever heard her talk that much to me before. "When I was little...I wanted you to hold me in your lap and...even when I was in the seventh and eighth grade...and getting too tall." Her voice almost gave way again, but she held onto it. "I wanted you to hug me and tell me you liked me...and maybe tell me that I was pretty because, because I knew I wasn't. I knew I was ugly." She stopped and I waited. "But if you told me I was okay, well...then what the kids said wouldn't have hurt so much." She was quiet for awhile and then, "Dad, are you listening?"

"Very much so, honey."

"Remember how I cried because the kids made fun of me then? Remember how they called me 'Bean Stalk?' "

I remember how when I was that age

44

the kids made fun of me and my strange clothes when we first came to America. My mother made me go to school in my English tweed suits until I finally confinced her that it was okay for me to wear sweaters and jeans like the other kids. I remember the kids calling me a Limey.

"And when they made fun of me," she explained, "I cried and I wanted you to put your arms around me. Did you know that?"

"I guess, honey, I just didn't think about it."

"I wanted you to hug me instead of giving me a lecture."

"But Catherine, you were a big girl then. Isn't it kind of foolish to be talking about this now."

She was silent for awhile and then she agreed. "Maybe it is," she said sadly. I had the odd feeling she was going to hang up. I tried to hang on to her.

"I don't know, honey, what you want me to say...or do. That's all in the past anyway. When you were...that 'Bean Stalk' business, wasn't that about junior high school?"

"Um-hummm."

"That's pretty old for...well, father's don't go around always hugging their

45

grown-up daughters," I laughed, trying to introduce some lightheartedness.

"Or even little daughters."

"You had to grow up, Catherine. Babying doesn't help anyone. Believe me, I know!"

How well I knew! If my parents had given in to my tears I never could have lasted at boarding school. My father had helped me to grow up the same way I helped Catherine.

When my father told me I was no longer a little boy, he had brought me into our study, a gloomy, book-filled room that no one seemed ever to enter. He shut the door and began what he called our "man-to-man" talk. In his business voice he explained it all to me.

"English gentlemen," he said, "start growing up when they're your age. From now on," he announced, "you are going to be living at the boarding school." I had known that when I turned eight years old this would happen, but each day after my eighth birthday I had prayed that some miracle would prevent it.

"When will I see you and Mum?" I asked, turning away from him so he wouldn't see the tears forming.

"Oh, holidays," he said. "We shall

come and fetch you every holiday."

I could hardly comprehend then what it would mean to be away from my family, but I knew I would miss them terribly. I would even miss my sister, though I fought with her every day. I wanted to tell my father, "I don't want to go. I want to live at home with Mum and Eileen and you. I don't want to live with boys I don't know." But I knew it would be no good to say anything. I would have to be strong, have to keep my chin up. The words I wanted to say to my father would not come out. They were not meant to.

My father told me what kind of a son he wanted. "You're eight years old now and this is the English way. You will be a brave young man and I will be proud of you." When he shook my hand I wanted to bury my face and cry into his scratchy vest. I wanted him to comfort me, though he never had.

Instead of crying in my father's arms, I cried myself to sleep in the boys' dormitory, muffling the sounds under my covers. I *knew* I wasn't the brave young man my father wanted to be proud of. Guilty of crying, I cried even more, ashamed of myself because I knew I would have disappointed my father.

It took me many months to learn to be brave, to smother my longing for my parents and my sister, to learn to repress my yearning. Only then could I earn back my self-respect.

When I became a father I was proud of myself that my child was not a baby. When Catherine cried because she thought she was a freak, as she called herself, I told her, "It's important to show the world a stiff upper lip. That way you'll earn respect of the people who ridicule you."

And the payoff of my "lectures," as she referred to my talks with her, came in her senior year at Burlingame High School in the middle of a packed football stadium at half-time when she was crowned Homecoming Queen. I presented her with a dozen, long-stemmed, red roses in front of the whole town.

"But Dad," Catherine interrupted my thoughts, "you and I ... I know I'm repeating myself, but what I need to find out is...why couldn't I go to you?"

"I don't know, honey. I don't see that that's so important...not *now* anyway. What's..."

"Dad, I'm trying to figure something

out. I've been wondering if the way you and I were . . . well if that has anything to do with . . . the way I relate to . . . to men."

"Oh, honey. You're stretching for something. We . . . you and I, we did just fine. Why when you were little I used to wheel you around the block, take you . . . take you to the zoo. And remember how often we all went to Disneyland?

"Sure I do, Dad. Every summer, and I loved that. But do you see what I'm talking about?"

"I don't know, honey. I guess so."

"Would you help me to understand it, Dad? It's important to me."

"Yes, honey. But . . . I don't know what you think your problem is. You're beautiful and men fall in love with you . . ."

"That's not it, Dad. There's something in me that holds me back. I think . . . I think there's something I reserve. I don't know. There's something I'm afraid of and I don't know what it is."

I thought for awhile and then asked, "Are you talking about sex?"

"No, Dad. That's not it either. I lived with Al, you know. Well, maybe you didn't know. I didn't want to disillusion you. And," her voice dropped, "I lived with Kevin for a year."

I didn't know what to say. What more did she want? What was it she had said about how she associated with men?

"Sounds like you've been associating okay," I said, kindly.

"No I haven't. I love Kevin and I wanted to spend my life with him, but he left. Oh, I know there were some things we didn't see eye-to-eye on...and some things that worried me about him."

"Like what?"

"Well, I don't want you to get mad at me like you did yesterday."

"The way I remember it, *you* were the one who got mad first." I laughed to let her know I wouldn't start that again if she didn't. "What worried you, honey?"

She took a long time to talk and then she spoke deliberately. "I worried about Kevin's drinking."

That hit me.

"He would take sips of whiskey out of the bottle whenever he was home. Wouldn't even pour it in a glass. Maybe I'm so worried that any guy I fall in love with will drink too much and that we'll split because of it...."

I listened.

"We talked about it once after a fight. He thought it wasn't that he drank that bothered me, but he said when he drank it reminded me of why you and Mom got a divorce. He said I saw *you* instead of him."

Old voices came back to me. My mind skipped back over about twenty-five years. Catherine's mother and I were standing in the kitchen. It was in the house we lived in after the girls were born. We had just put them to bed, babies in their cribs. I remember we were arguing in whispers so we wouldn't wake them.

"I wouldn't care if you drank a gallon a day," Lisa whispered, "if it didn't change you. You draw away from me. You get mean. I don't dare talk to you because you misinterpret what I say. So I draw into myself and then I get lonely."

I explained to her that she must know the pressure I was under on my job. My God, it was almost more than I could stand! Sometimes I felt I wanted to blow up the whole I.B.M. building, get everybody off my back, or run away, disappear, change my name. And my wife, instead of helping me, here she was harping on me about my drinking. It was the only release I had and she'd take that away from me. Couldn't she see that all this pressure was for her and the kids! So I tried to tell her about her own peculiar bias bout my drinking.

"When I drink, Lisa," I explained patiently, "you relate that to my mother's drinking, and because she was an alcoholic you're seeing me as an..."

"That's not true," she whispered. "I see you. I don't even think about your mother."

That couldn't be true. I saw my mother. I couldn't get the pictures of my mother's drunken orgies out of my mind. Always I would have the picture in my mind of that time in England when I was only six years old and she had told me I could have a tea party.

That was the time that I made my own invitations and the neighbor's children came to my upstairs playroom where mother had let me spread out her good linen. Our maid had helped me rearrange the room for the party. I was excited because it was my first party. There was no way I could have known that it would be my last.

My friends arrived in their best British style suits with the wide collars and we giggled nervously while we waited for mother to bring the tea tray. She had dismissed our maid because she said this was going to be "our" party. I had felt very close to my mother when we were making the plans. Dad was away as usual and we were being independent.

In the morning my mother and I had prepared the crumpets and spaced them around on the big silver tray. She poured me a glass of my favorite cherry juice to drink while we got things ready. She was drinking pineapple juice.

We moved around the kitchen, finding delicacies the children would like. We carefully lined the little bone china cups and saucers in a row for mother to bring to the upstairs playroom later, after the party started. We laughed and planned together like a couple of conspirators. And when the time was right, the children arrived and we all traipsed upstairs while mother put the finishing touches on the food.

My friends and I played with my toys for a long while, all of us waiting for the real point of the party, which of course was the tray full of sweet crumpets. We waited and played and waited some more and then we finally heard my mother slowly coming up the stairs. She fumbled with the door knob. We were all very anxious. Then I heard a piece of china fall to the floor and break. I ran to the door to help her.

I had never seen my mother look the way she did. She stood at the door, wobbling, with the large tray askew, trying to balance the porcelain tea pot, the thin cups and saucers, and the plate of crumpets. I thought at first her trouble was that the tray was too big for her. She was used to having maids do this kind of service. But then I saw her hair hanging down in big hunks with her hair pins dangling, and her eyes didn't seem to be going where the dishes were going. When a cup slid to one side of the tray, her eyes stayed where the cup had been after the cup had slid to the other side.

"I'll help you, Mum," I offered, reaching to balance the tray. It crashed to the floor. The other children gasped and ran over to watch the liquid seep into the carpet, and the crumpets change from their fluffy cream color to a soggy brown. I reached down to save something, but there was nothing to save. I simply looked at the pile of broken china.

My mother yelled at me. "*You* did

this!'' Slurring words I had never heard before, she damned me, my father, England, and all the neighbors whose children fled down the stairs and out the front door, followed by her venomous accusations of having come from familes that thought they were better than she was. I sat down on the floor and cried. I think my mother went back downstairs to the kitchen, probably to drink more pineapple juice that must have been mostly gin. And in the years that followed, even though I still missed her when I was away at boarding school, and loved her for a long time before I learned to hate her, I never could believe in her again.

As I grew up I collected other photographs of her in my mind. Though they were the kind I wanted to discard, they were like things that stubbornly stick to your fingers, that you can't shake off.

I don't know how many different pictures my memory has stored up of my mother, year after year, climbing the stairs to the second floor of our house at the end of the day, so drunk she could hardly hang on to the banister. I can see her now, how she would squint her glassy eyes to focus on me or on the stairs. By evening her black hair would have fallen out of her hair pins, hanging limp, making her look like a witch. When she would try to maneuver each one of the many stairs, I would worry about her falling back down. When I was little I was afraid she would hurt herself and I wanted to help her. When I grew up I hoped she'd fall and kill herself.

In the morning scenes she would open her bedroom door with a flourish and descend the stairs with her head up and eyes straight ahead, steady on her feet. Her hair would be perfectly arranged, and her clothes would be neat and pretty. In the kitchen she would go about getting breakfast cheerfully with no memory of the night before. No matter how vicious she had been in the evening, when morning came the slate was wiped clean — for her.

I used to hope that the transformation from evening witch to my morning-nice mother would be the precious omen signalling the beginning of our family's life without drunkenness. But it was morning hope against evening despair and it was the evening that came back strongest. Though I was always disappointed, it still took years for me to accept the fact that I could not trust the future of any situation that included my mother. And though she no longer exists, the pictures haunt my mind. So when I said to Lisa that when Lisa looked at me she saw my mother, I knew what I was talking about. She must have seen my mother. My God, I sure do!

But now, all these years later...here is this boy, Kenneth? Kevin, telling Catherine she looked at him...and saw me? No, that's too far-fetched. I told Catherine firmly, "There is no way he, or you, or anyone can compare you and me, or me and my mother."

"Dad, I don't know what you're talking about. I never knew your mother, remember? I'm not talking about you and your mother. I'm talking about Kevin. And I'm worried about his drinking. But I think I'm...I'm afraid that when people drink a lot..."

"They'll become alcoholics. I know that line. God knows I heard it often enough from your mother."

"Well...maybe this is not the time to talk about that. It's not the reason I needed to talk with you anyway."

What was the reason? My mind had been wandering. Ah, yes, Catherine's boyfriend.

"You know, honey, I'm sorry this boy, Kevin, left, if you really wanted him to stick around. But give him a couple of days." I looked at the clock on the kitchen wall, getting nervous that Betty might be waking up.

"No. It's... it's over," Catherine said.

"There will be others."

"Hmmmm. And will I have the same problem?" She didn't seem to be asking a question.

"Problem? I don't think you have a problem, honey."

"I'm beginning to think I do. That's why I wanted to talk to you. But... I guess... holding back something... or keeping a distance... I can see now, I don't think you know you do it."

"Do what, for Christ sake, Catherine? What is it you think I do?" This was beginning to irritate me. I felt we had been going around in circles.

"Don't get cross," she said to me curtly. I didn't like that. She reminded me of her mother. Or was it *my* mother?

"I'm not cross, and I don't... what was it you said?"

"Keep a distance. You keep a distance."

"Of course I keep a distance, as you call it. If I understand your meaning, I don't cozy up to just anybody."

"I know. You don't cozy up...even to your own family."

"You're right!" I was getting impatient. "Where do you think you'd be right now if I had molly-coddled you?" I was shouting at her. I might wake up Betty, so I softened my voice. "Do you think I was going to have a couple of 'cry babies?'" I thought for a moment. "Instead of being critical of me, and I think you *are* being critical, Catherine, instead of being critical because I didn't hug you, as you keep saying, just thank God I didn't."

"Dad, don't get upset," she said, "I'll work it out...some other way."

"Yes...well...It's time for Betty to be getting up anyway."

"I'm glad I called, Dad. I think I've learned what...what I needed to know."

"I don't know, honey. Anyway, I'm going to have to hang up now. After all, it's Sunday, you know, and I have to get ready to go to Mass. If we hurry we can make the twelve-thirty."

Catherine was silent. I probably shouldn't have mentioned going to Mass. My returning to the church was a sore point with Lisa and the girls. Something about the bishop asking Lisa to sign an annulment so Betty and I could get married by the priest. That had made Lisa angry. She refused to sign the annulment and that delayed things a bit.

"Aren't all days Sundays?" Catherine asked. "Now that you're retired?"

"Yes, now that you mention it. And Cathy, about that problem you think you have. You're okay. You're my girl, and you know your own mind. You're strong. You'll live through this Kevin thing. We all go through something like this at least once in our life. And Cathy...I want you to know, I'm proud of you. You know that?"

That was the one thing I'd always wanted my father to tell *me*.

"Thanks, Dad. That's the first time you said that. Thanks."

"Forget about that problem. If you think you're keeping a distance, well, there's nothing wrong with that."

"I don't know," she said before we hung up. "I'm beginning to think... maybe there *is* something wrong with that... and I'm beginning to think, also, it might be...in a way...it might be hereditary."

Chapter 3

"Daughter"

Glen was my brother. Not really. Not a birth brother, but maybe more than that. When Kevin walked out on me I telephoned Glen right after I phoned my mother because calling Glen was a natural thing to do.

"He's gone," I said, trying not to cry until I could explain more. "He left. Walked out. I don't understand..." and then the tears started again and I couldn't speak. I could hear Glen talking but I couldn't answer him. And anyway, I didn't agree with him.

"He didn't deserve you, Doll," Glen was saying. "You're ten times a better person..." I just shook my head and sobbed into the phone, my heart and mind telling me that I wasn't any "ten times better." I couldn't have been. If that were true, Kevin wouldn't have left.

Only ten minutes ago, as though it would be forever, Kevin was right here in the small house we shared together in the Hollywood hills. I wondered what had happened to the two people we were then, when we rented this cottage a year ago. I remembered the fun we had when we finished this place with hand-down furniture from our friends and second-hand stores. How happy we were when we left this cottage each morning for our respective law clerk jobs to anticipate coming together again at the end of the day. Now, for whatever reason I couldn't understand, Kevin was probably at this very moment pulling onto the freeway in his VW Bug, moving away from all of this at sixty miles an hour. In a matter of a few minutes, Kevin and I had torn our love affair apart, accusing each other of not trying hard enough to make things work.

"You don't care about us," I'd said when he walked in at eight o'clock, too late for the movie I'd wanted both of us to see. "All you care about is work, work, work! You stay at your office until it's *safe* to come home, until you're sure it's too late for us to do something together."

He set his brief case on the floor, thoughtful. "I intend to make something of myself," he told me. I realized he had not reached for me as he usually did when he came home. I knew then he was in one of his cold moods. "I don't agree with your philosophy, making just enough money to get by, so we can have more time together. If you could understand how I feel..."

"Understand? Kevin..." I'd attempted one more time, "I don't want to hold you back. *I* want success too. It's just that..." I wondered why I was trying. We'd been through this so many times before.

In our first months we couldn't get *enough* time together. Kevin had cut some of his law school classes to be with me, and he had left his law clerk job a full ten minutes early to be waiting for me when I got off work. In our plans for our future we talked of setting up a law firm together with the understanding that *time* with each other was the most important thing.

When we first started living together we were inseparable. For both of us life had a newness. We saw things together through the eyes of our love for each other. In the freshness and the confidence of our love we experimented, doing things we'd never done before. We explored new ways to make love, we cooked new recipes, and rearranged the furniture to make it fit "us." We painted the porch, changing the color from a battleship grey to a bright yellow, bicycled in the early dawn, read the Sunday papers until noon and then returned to bed to make love again.

We jogged in the mornings to watch the sunrise at the beach, and in the evenings we went back again to see the sun set. We stretched the fun of life as fully as we could. And because we loved what we did together, we loved each other more. I felt a completeness I had not known I could feel. I had never dreamed that anyone so full of happiness could ever again be unhappy. It was to be forever...until it all began to change.

At first it was so gradual it was like a fog that creeps in at the end of a warm, sunny day. What had happened to that good feeling? I thought it must be a mistake, that I was simply imagining that Kevin was changing. When he seemed distant to me I tried to ignore that. "Don't be so sensitive," I scolded myself. But it happened too often to be my imagination.

Then it had all come down to this, when just a few minutes ago we started saying some of the harsh things that were becoming a habit with us. But this time I recognized a difference. This time the accusations were the same but there was a conviction in Kevin's voice I had not heard before. Without putting words to it then, I saw later that what we were really doing was disguising our "good-byes."

"There's too much difference," Kevin had said.

I couldn't understand that. It made me cry. I loved him. What did I care about "difference?" *What* difference? Hadn't our love brought us close...so close, I reminded him, that we had almost become one person.

"That was months ago," he said, wistfully.

"We've drifted apart a little...that's true...but at times," I groped, "we've been like we used to be."

But it was no use. I couldn't keep down a surge of hopelessness. He would not let himself be persuaded. My love could no longer touch him. Yet I continued to plead. I felt my life slipping away and I was helpless. When I knew that I had begged enough and there was no use, I gave up.

"You might as well leave," I tried, the tears running down my face. "I don't want you here to...to torture me." And I let go of thoughts I'd never put to words before. "I don't want your back turned to me in bed anymore." Those memories brought a new rush of tears. "I touch you ...in the night and,...you wince. Did you know that? And I wait for you to come home at night. When I'm at work I can't wait for the last hour of the day to end so I can get home. Then I wait for you. And maybe you come at six o'clock. Or seven. I wonder," I said, my tears beginning to subside, "I wonder why I care so much, when...when you don't."

"I care, Cath," he said, and he began to reach out to me and then he pulled back. "I care," he repeated looking away from me.

"But not enough," I said, getting better control of myself. "You might as well leave, Kevin," I said. "There's no point in our living together anymore."

"I know." He picked up his brief case and stepped to the door, as though he had waited for this cue. He turned back. "I'm going to Steve's. I'll get my stuff... tomorrow when you're not here...." He looked at me and dropped his brief case.

Then he reached out for me and held me in his arms. For a moment I felt my life flood back into my body. He kissed me and told me that he loved me. I suddenly knew everything was going to be all right after all.

Then he left.

The door closed and I stood there listening to his footsteps going down the stairs. I heard his car start and move out of hearing. I was surrounded in silence.

Everything I had wanted had moved away from my life. The silence, the aloneness, was more than I could bear. I had to touch base with something...with someone. That was when I talked to my mother and after that with Glen.

"You're my port in this storm, just as always, Glen."

After I explained what had happened he told me, "You'll be okay, Doll, you're okay. You know that. It will be rough for awhile, but...things will get better."

I had no words for that. I couldn't see that far ahead.

"You there?" he asked after my long silence.

"Um mmmm," I mumbled.

"You know," he said, "I was always worried about the onesidedness of your love for Kevin."

"Um mmmm," I mumbled again.
Glen had told me that before. I was sure
he was filling up the time with things to
say, to help me.

"You worried too much about
Kevin," he said.

"Worried?" I sniffled. That I hadn't
heard before. "How do you mean?"

"Remember when you were going
with Al?"

"Yes." That seemed so long ago.

"Did you ever worry about what he
thought about you?"

"Well, I don't know...."

"And Jack? Did you worry what he
thought?"

"Not really."

"But Kevin. You worried about Kevin.
All the time you worried. Do you see the
difference? You were always asking... if
he would like something you bought...
something you planned for him, or... do
you see?"

"Yes. I couldn't tell, I mean, when we
first lived together, I felt I could tell,
when he was happy with me. But..." I
tried to get hold of my crying again,
"Lately it seemed he didn't want me to
make him happy. Then I'd try harder to

do little things and...Oh, I don't know...
I was always afraid he wouldn't like..."

"That's it!" And he went on talking
while my mind drifted. "You worked too
hard at it," he said.

"Hm mmmm," I agreed. It had been
so delicate. I had been "walking on
eggs," fearful that I would say or do
something that would make them break.

"I worried about you," Glen repeated.

I had known that too. Glen could tell
by looking at me, sitting in law school at
night, how things were with Kevin. I
would try to mask my feelings, but Glen
knew me too well.

"You know," he went on, "when
Kevin worked all day Saturdays and Sundays, I wondered what he thought about
you and me...when we went to the
movies."

"Kevin knew we were just friends," I
said. "He didn't get jealous."

"Maybe not jealous in the usual way.
But I think it bothered him. It probably
didn't do your love life any good."

Glen's suspicions were right. When
Kevin came home from work late on a
Saturday evening and I told him I'd gone
to the matinee ballet with Glen, he was
sullen for awhile, poured himself a couple

of quick bourbon drinks and then said he thought it was not wise for me to "cavort with queers."

I thought he just must be referring to the ballet performers, because many male dancers are known to be homosexuals. "I'm not cavorting with them, silly," I said. "I just watched them. The dancing was beautiful."

"You know what I'm talking about," he said.

He waited, expecting something from me. I watched him and I saw how the drinks changed him. The liquor seemed to let his anger out and there was a different tone in his voice. Things he would say when he was not drinking, sounded cutting, harmful, with the alcohol.

"I mean Glen," he said.

Now we were in it. I could ignore him, or I could argue with him. Either way was a losing way for both of us. Kevin didn't like Glen. He would never like Glen, no matter how much I defended him. I fumbled with ideas...wondering what to do. I decided to try avoiding his meaning.

"I know you don't like Glen," I said, "but...I like having someone...harmless ...to do things with while you're working

72

on Saturdays and Sundays. Kevin, do you have to work so much?" There, without planning it, I turned the conversation on to another tack.

"Yes. I have to work if I want to get ahead."

Well, I had headed off an argument, but that was all. Now he'd retreat to his silent self and I'd wait, maybe for days, before he'd speak to me again with any kind of warmth.

At these times I was grateful for my friendship with Glen. Through the weeks of alternating gloom and sunshine, it had been Glen who had kept my spirits up.

"You're my best friend," I often told him. But really we were more like brother and sister who've known when to laugh at the same old family jokes, and what is off-limits for humor. Always on the safe side of sarcasm, Glen never made fun of people, not even of Kevin, though he probably wanted to, especially if he thought it might cheer me up.

My life with Kevin had been changing for some time. After his law school classes he'd stay at work late at night and then he'd go back to the law office on Saturdays, and as time passed, on most Sundays too.

Once I told him I thought his boss was using him. "Fisher depends on you as a law firm partner depends on another partner, not as a senior usually depends on a law clerk. Even though I knew that might make him angry, I wanted to make my point. "Fisher flatters you and his flattery gets you to turn out volumes of work. Flattery gets him seven days a week of your labor for practically nothing. And...and we never have time to be together like we used to."

"I wish you'd quit nagging that point. I'm getting valuable experience. It may not pay now, but some day..."

"*Some* day," I said, "some day is *now*! We're alive *now*! You're always postponing the time we're going to spend together. You're so dedicated to the future you can't see the present. I love you and we're living together *now*," I pleaded.

"But sweetheart, try to be patient. I love you too, but we're not living the way I want it," he said. "I want us to be more established."

"Established?" I said, and then we were off on another argument. I thought he was going to leave then. Now I wondered if his leaving had been inevitable.

I had seen our love affair disintegrating and I didn't know what to do. The feeling of completeness I had at the beginning was disappearing. I used to compare that wholeness of our love to a large, round beautiful stone. But then I could see that when something hits a stone it can be weakened. And if something else hits it, and the weak spot falls out, then we have lost something. Then, when the stone is no longer whole, something else hits it, and another part is chipped, and another. The weaker it gets, the more vulnerable it is to further damage so that it is easily split and crumbles away.

My efforts to repair the early damage, never really sure what caused it, seemed to work at first. I'd do something like cook beef stroganoff, or ask Kevin's friend, Steve, to come over and bring his wife and baby. That always made Kevin happy.

Or I tried other things, like suggesting a camping trip, but the things that worked best were setting up short "get-togethers" with Kevin's old friends. Buying a case of beer and inviting his law school friends over to watch the Rose Bowl game for instance. Things like that did make a difference. Kevin would relax and laugh and he would be warmer toward me.

I would have given anything if I could get us back to the beginning, if we could have started all over. I often dwelt on memories of how we were when we first met...how different we were. I remember how proud I was of him when we first started going together.

Kevin was the man I could look up to, someone who was, well, above me in ways I couldn't describe. I liked the way he moved through a party. I liked his natural sun-tanned blondness. He always knew what to wear. He could pick up on so many subjects and I admired his social poise.

I remember, too, that at first he was as nice at home as he was at parties, or when we were out by ourselves together. But that, too, began to change. I saw that there was what I began to tell myself, the "social" man and the "private" man, and they were different.

One time, only six months ago, at Fisher's reception for his daughter's engagement, Kevin was his "social" best. I loved the pride I felt in him. His suit with the vest, his new hair style, his perfect manners, his knowing what to say to everyone, all those things brought back the old surge of adoration. He was in an "up" mood and I loved it.

His good mood continued on the way home and he suggested that we stop at one of our old favorite spots. We danced together, laughed together, and later at home, we made love together as we used to.

The next morning I woke up late, the rays of the sun already spread across the blankets of our bed. It was Sunday and I was happy in the way I used to be. I rolled over to caress Kevin, but his side of the bed was empty. I went into the front room where he was writing, a clip-board on his lap, and I kissed him with the passion of the night before.

He did not respond. I wondered what I had done wrong.

"Good morning," he said and his slim smile let me know that I had inconveniently interrupted him.

"I'm sorry," I said.

"That's okay, sweetheart," he said, taking my hand. "It's, I have to get this in to Fisher by ten o'clock."

"This morning? It's *Sunday*!"

"No matter. I have to keep going."

I was closed out — put aside, to be

reckoned with later. I had wanted to be important to him as he was to me, but gradually I was relegated to a second or third place, waiting on the outskirts of his life for periodic small attentions he could afford to spend on me.

The feeling of being put aside was not new. When I was little I used to wait for the few times my father could spend any time with me. My mother used to tell me it wasn't because Daddy didn't love me; it was that he had that important job. I hoped then that when I grew up the man who loved me would always put me in first place. No job would be more important than our love.

What a childish wish!

I remembered how the teachers of my elementary school had beamed on me when my father accepted the presidency of their P.T.A. "You should be proud of your father," Mrs. Thorsen told me. "Not many men as important as your father would take time for our P.T.A."

I told my mother about that comment and we were both glad about what Mrs. Thorsen said. But I'm sure we also knew that this would cut down on my father's time at home.

But then when I got older, even when

my father *was* home, I didn't want to get near him when he'd have that glassy look in his eyes after drinking a lot. At those times he'd be mean for no reason, so Anne and I stayed out of his way. It seemed that almost anything was more important to my father than I was. His job, his community manipulations, and later his drinking. I was put in a safe second or third place and it hurt, just as it hurt to be in a second or third place with Kevin.

If I'd wanted to be just the housewife type I knew I wouldn't be having this problem. But being equal was important to me.

"Women's Liberation?" Kevin had asked, half in jest when we agreed to live together. "*I* do half the housework?"

"It's only fair," I answered. "I work too. I go to school too."

"Okay, but I'm not going to cook."

"Why not? You *eat.*" He didn't like that. I softened it. "I didn't know much about cooking until I moved away from home. It's fun. Here," I brought out a couple of ragged-eared cookbooks. "I used to go through these and see what sounded good."

He didn't smile.

"I made some messes," I told him. "Threw stuff away, but not much anymore." He didn't say anything. "I'll cook the first week."

"Well, I'll try," he said. At first I thought he was leary of failing in the kitchen, but later I realized he thought it would be demeaning because, as he told me, "My Dad never would have done this."

Nevertheless he tried. One Saturday morning after he had put together a stew and had also learned to operate the washing machine, he flopped down in one of our living room chairs and laughed, "If my father could see me now!"

When he first started helping, the things he learned to do around the house were interesting for him because he had never done them before. "I don't mind the cooking," he confessed. "It's even kind of fun. But I'd sure hate to have to do it all the time."

Then the novelty began to wear off. I felt he resented me when he was pushing the vacuum cleaner, or when it was his time to defrost the refrigerator. But if I took over and did it all I knew I'd resent him.

He'd probably still be here, I told myself, if I'd just done all the work.

Through all those thoughts that flashed by in seconds I could now and then hear Glen's voice talking to me on the telephone, but I hadn't been listening. Then I heard him ask, "Do you want me to come over?"

"No," I answered. I tried to concentrate on him. "Thank you anyway, Glen. I just wanted to talk to you. I thought maybe you'd understand why Kevin left. You've seen it all. I don't...I can't figure it out. Even though we argued, we loved each other."

"I don't know why he left, Cath. All I know is I hate to see you hurt." Then he paused and added, hopefully, "Maybe he'll drive around awhile and come back."

"Do you think so? No...he's gone. I know that. I think he's been leaving me for weeks. But tonight it really happened."

"Did he tell you *before* that he was leaving?"

"No, but I could tell. He's been different. Like he was getting himself ready to tell me. I don't understand."

"Well, what happened, exactly?" I told him all about it again.

"And yet I know that he loves me, Glen. That's what I don't understand. Why did he have to leave?"

"I don't know, Doll. I don't know. I'm sorry you're hurt. I really am. When you're hurt, I'm hurt. Want me to come over?"

"No, I'll be okay. I feel better. Really, I do."

"I'll just hang on here until I *know* you're okay."

"I'm okay. I'm confused. But I'm okay. I wanted to talk with you. I called my Mom. She's coming down day after tomorrow. But you *know* Kevin. I thought talking with you about it might help me understand. I'll let you go now, Glen. I'll get off the phone."

"I'll see you tomorrow night in class. Be there?"

"Yes. I'll be there. I'll be all right." But when he mentioned tomorrow I wondered how I was going to face it. I tried to picture myself getting up out of bed — a bed I'd slept in the whole night by myself. I saw myself making coffee for one person instead of for two. Then I was scanning the morning paper with no one to share the news. I was dressing and then I was leaving for work in the terrible silence of living alone, knowing Kevin would be starting *his* first day alone, from Steve's apartment.

Steve and Kevin were no doubt discussing me right now. I could almost hear the conversation. I knew that Steve did not approve of me. I knew he liked me when we first met, but after one particular discussion, his attitude toward me changed.

We had been talking about Steve and Sandy's little boy, Tommy. I had just been playing with him and had said how much they must love their little boy.

"He's our *life!*" Sandy had said, picking him up and cuddling him in her arms.

Steve looked at his wife and then at Tommy and said his son was the pride of his life. "I look at Tommy and I *know* I've got to make something of myself. I want him to be proud of his dad. Having children makes life really worthwhile. It's in God's plan."

I saw Steve's and Kevin's eyes meet. "God's plan," I said to myself. I remembered seeing a crucifix over Tommy's crib and I recalled Kevin's discussion about when he "used to be a Catholic." When Steve and Kevin looked at each other like that, something — some knowing, passed between them. That look between them isolated me and it made me angry.

"My life," I said, "is not vacant, though I don't intend to either marry or to have children." No one said anything. "Life," I continued, "*is* worthwhile for me without that."

I saw Sandy stiffen.

"I think it's good," I continued, "that people choose to marry and choose to have children." Sandy smiled at me. "I think it's good that those who choose not to, can still..."

"It's not natural for people to make *that* choice," Steve interrupted, lifting Tommy from Sandy's lap and tossing him into the air, talking to him and laughing loudly each time Tommy laughed. I started to speak again, but it was clear that Steve had closed the conversation. I kept quiet.

Kevin and I had talked of my thoughts on marriage and children before, but my actually saying these things to Steve made a difference to Kevin. I guess he hadn't wanted Steve to know my ideas. After that evening there was a barrier between Steve and me. Whenever the four of us were together, no matter how jovial I was, or how much effort I made, Steve could hardly talk to me.

"Steve treats me as though...just because I don't want what *he* wants, that I'm a...a 'weirdo!' " I told Kevin.

"Sweetheart, you're no 'weirdo,' " he reassured me. And because he was in one of his good moods, he pulled me to him and one loving evening erased a week of agonizing over what Steve thought and how that would affect Kevin.

"Why do I get the feeling that he thinks I'm abnormal?" I asked Kevin.

"He's been raised differently than you. He's been raised Catholic."

"So were you," I reminded him.

"Yes. But I left the church. And also, sweetheart, remember, he's not in love with you, and I am." With just a few words, Kevin gave me back my world. "Even though Steve's my best friend," he said, "you're my best girl friend, my love, and we're not going to let him get in our way."

If only that had been true. Kevin could make love to me, but it was Steve's ideas that he accepted. And right now he was not in our home, he was in Steve's.

At other times when we had arguments, Kevin had gone to Steve's. It was always after we had arguments about the future. When Kevin talked about marriage I told him flatly, as I had before, that I didn't want to get married.

"But if you love me," he'd say, "why won't you marry me?"

"I *do* love you, very much."

"I don't see how you can really love me if you won't marry me."

"Why does one necessarily go with the other?" I asked.

"It's just natural."

"Now you sound like Steve," I smiled.

"Look, sweetheart, I love you. What do you have against marriage?"

"Nothing," I answered. "I just don't have anything *for* it. Look at us. We've lived together for a year. We were perfectly happy, I would even say, ecstatically happy, until you mentioned marriage. Why couldn't we have gone on as we were?"

"It's not the way I want to live my life," he answered. Then, frustrated, he would leave our house and go talk to Steve, returning hours later.

Now, once again, Kevin had gone to Steve's, but this time there was a finality I had never sensed before. It was in the way he held me and kissed me before he left.

If Kevin had gone to Fred's apartment, or to Mike's, I might have felt more hope for his return. Their single lifestyle would put Kevin on his own. He would have to share in buying the groceries, he'd have to help with the cooking, and if he wanted to be entertained he'd have to help arrange that. But at Steve's, his emotional wounds would be soothed, his clothes would be washed by Steve's wife, and his meals would be cooked for him. He would only need to sit back and receive the warmth of their concern and he would of course hear what he wanted to hear.

"You've done the right thing," Steve would say.

When Kevin had returned from Steve's before, many months ago, he had told me of conversations much like one that was probably going on now.

"You were brought up to look forward to marriage and a family," Steve told him. "It goes against the grain to walk down a path that leads nowhere. You want to visualize a future with children, watching them develop just like we see Tommy here. We spend hours watching him and thinking about what he's going to be."

"I agreed with Steve," Kevin told me when he returned.

"When we first started to live together," I reminded him, "nothing was said about marriage. We simply loved each other."

"I assumed we would get..."

"Married? Kevin, thousands of couples are living together these days without being married. It's no *sin* anymore."

He shook his head. I persisted. "Why is it wrong for you, when the whole country accepts it?"

"I'm not the whole country. It's, maybe I'm the peculiar one-in-a-thousand. I happen to want to get married. I almost...almost *did*," he admitted.

"You *did?* When?"

"Recently. We were planning on getting married last January."

"January? We only met in April!" When we had met he had not appeared broken-hearted, or...on the rebound.

"I know. I broke it off before Christmas. It was hard to do, but I didn't love her enough. Oh...I loved her, I thought then. But there was something missing. I don't know. It wasn't right."

"It is hard to break up, even if you don't love the other person." I spoke from my own experience.

"It was very hard for her," he said. "She cried. She couldn't understand it. She had thought I wanted to get married. And I *had*, but I had to get out of it."

"Why?"

"I think...I thought about it a lot. I think it was because I didn't feel it was *my* decision in the first place."

"How do you mean? She suggested it?"

"No. The church. I had always been taught, if you sleep with a woman, you do it *after* marriage. Oh, I know we all do it, but that doesn't mean I didn't feel guilty about it."

"Guilty! Do you feel guilty sleeping with *me*?"

"Ours is different. Different than with Joan. With you I don't think about guilty ...not very often."

"But you *do* feel guilty?"

"Not as much as I used to with Joan. I think because she was Catholic too. And her parents belonged to the same parish."

"And," I groped, "because I'm not Catholic, you don't..."

"The difference between Joan and you has nothing to do with the church."

"Did she...were you the one...Oh, hell, I hate to think of you making love to someone else, but I know it happened, just as you know you're not *my* first lover, but why should people feel guilty? I don't feel guilty."

"I know. That helps me."

"I have no religion," I told him. I didn't want anything unsaid to stand between us.

"Neither do I, now, since I've gotten away from the church. When I broke off with Joan, I couldn't go to church. I didn't want to see her there. And anyway, it made me feel guilty that I'd broken up with her, and I'd had sex with her. I was her first one. I did it when I thought we were going to get married. I felt awful, later."

"And now?"

"I try not to think about it."

He was silent for a long time before he told me, "I never really did love Joan. I know that now. I thought I did. But since I've met you, there's no comparison. There's also no reason why...since

90

we *do* love each other...no reason why we shouldn't get married."

I thought we'd been over that often enough so I didn't say anything more.

"No reason," he said, "unless you don't want to make the commitment."

"Commitment!" I said. "I've *made* the commitment! I *love* you! I *love* you! Don't you understand? Isn't that *enough*?"

His silence was my answer.

"You really mean it?" he asked.

"That I love you? Of course I..."

"No. You know what I mean. You really mean it that you don't want to get married?"

"Yes, but that doesn't mean I don't love you." I went to him and sat in his lap and kissed his blonde, curly hair, his ears, his forehead. He was unresponsive. I pretended not to notice, confident that I could bring his passion to the surface. I kissed his lips that refused to soften and pressed myself to his rigid body. Then he kissed me quickly, squeezed me abruptly and moved me off his lap.

He stood up.

I had been dismissed.

During that next week he was quiet. He seldom smiled or offered any conversation, though he would answer me if I asked him a question. It was at about that time that he began to stay even longer at work. Then, when it would seem that his mood had run its course, he would come home all smiles, and with newsy talk. We would enjoy life together once more. It was like we were finding each other all over again.

But our happiness couldn't hold. We would have several good weeks and then he'd start sliding down into one of his gloomy spells. I never knew specifically what triggered his wide swings of mood, but it was always some way related to a reference to our life in the future.

He would unexpectedly get quiet and then as the days passed, he would get depressed. It would take me sometimes a whole week to trace the process back and pin-point the conversation where we, for instance, might have been talking about when we would be full-fledged attorneys. At those times I didn't realize that he had very likely seen himself either "living in sin," as he referred to our life together, or living, sadly, without me.

Or maybe he knew all along, after he was sure about my feelings on marriage, that it was just a matter of time before

he would have to leave. Where living together had made me feel complete, I
could see now, it made Kevin feel empty.

I wondered how much he *had* thought
about the girl he almost married, and if
he thought about the times that he had
sex with her. I wondered if he thought
about his leaving the church, and I wondered about all those things in his back-
ground and how they had all come down
to this moment, to the moment of his
leaving.

I felt that he couldn't stay with me
because of all those many things that had
nothing to do with me. Were all of the
things that had gone on before me in his
life my enemy? And what of the things
that had gone on in *my* life before Kevin?
Were they *his* enemy?

All these past months I had been trying to decipher Kevin, and I had not
looked at myself. I thought because I was
free and liberated that I was a clear, open
page, but I began to question that.

Smug and secure I had said, ''I didn't
need marriage.'' But maybe I was fearful
that marriage would take something
away.

I don't know why, but I thought of
my father again. In my mind I saw him

when I was a little girl. Tears came to my eyes as I remembered him when I had wanted to crawl up on his lap, to snuggle into his arms.

"Daddy," I had wanted to say when I was little, "please hold me. Pick me up on your lap." But all I could do was form the words in my mind. I couldn't bring myself to ask him.

I saw myself in the dream I was creating, standing before my father, wanting to get the words out, to make them reach him, but the words stayed in my mouth, and in my heart. My father sat in his big, brown leather chair and continued to read his paper.

"Daddy," I tried.

"Yes, Catherine," he said from behind his paper.

"Daddy?"

He didn't answer me.

I recognized this dream. I had had it often when I was little. Only then it wasn't a dream. I loved my father and I knew he loved me, but there was some reason he couldn't tell me he loved me. There was some reason he couldn't pick me up. Some reason he couldn't hold me. I know he was always busy, but this was something more. Was it because he was above me? Was that why we could never feel close? Why had I always felt unworthy of him?

I needed to know these things. I needed to know about my father and me. There was something there that had to do with Kevin and me. Maybe some distance that made me hold something back. Maybe Kevin was right, that I *hadn't* made a commitment.

I wondered if I could, after all these years, talk to my father about this. Could I even try? Could I lift the curtain he put between us...between himself and everybody? Was the curtain of his drinking something he drew in front of himself so nobody could really see him? Was *he* afraid of something? Was *I* afraid of something? Afraid of the commitment that Kevin spoke of? If my father had never made a commitment to me, was I ...getting back at him through the men I knew? If he couldn't ever hug me, then had he really accepted me?

If I could talk to him, maybe...just maybe I could get him to talk to me. Maybe I could find out how we were. I would have to try. Tomorrow I would phone him. I would try.

"You okay?" Glen asked still on the phone.

"Yes," I answered slowly. Once again his voice brought me out of the past and I knew I would have to really think about the present, and worse that that, the awful future of tomorrow. I saw before me the people I would meet, those I worked with during the day, and the students at law school in the evening. I knew that it would show all over my face that Kevin had left me. And if anyone mentioned Kevin, I was sure that I would break down and cry.

"You're going to be all right, you know that," Glen told me one more time. "You'll be all right," he insisted. I felt he had followed my thoughts.

"I know...I hope so, Glen. Thanks for helping me. I'll say goodbye now. I know I'll live." I tried to laugh. "Tomorrow. See you tomorrow." I hung up.

I'll live, I told myself. I'll go through the motions. I'll talk and I'll smile. I'll even jog and maybe eventually go dancing. And people may never know that inside I will be dead.

When I set the phone back on its cradle I wandered slowly through our small house. I felt Kevin's presence everywhere and I saw all his things. They had no significance for me before, but now they all stood out, emphasizing his absence.

I looked at his clothes in the closet hanging next to mine. I walked into the bathroom and saw his razor and toothbrush sitting on the wash stand. They echoed his words, "I'm going to Steve's. I'll get my stuff tomorrow when you're not here."

I walked back into the bedroom and saw his open book by our bed, marking the spot where I interrupted his reading last night when I coaxed him into making love. I saw his soiled laundry waiting on the top of the washer, even his bicycle pump hanging on the door of the service porch, and they all had something different about them now. Before, they had been casual additions to Kevin's existence. Now, they were all substitutes for him, all that was left of a year of our life together. And tomorrow these, too, would be gone.

I re-walked through the house. I touched his clothes in the closet, his razor in the bathroom. I held his shoes in my hands and cried over them, cherishing their presence, wanting to hold them and love them as I wanted to hold and love their owner. I looked at all these objects as of one who had died.

Then a different thing happened. They suddenly repulsed me. I dropped his shoes. These were not the possessions left behind by a beloved deceased. These were things that belonged to a man who was looking for some kind of fulfillment away from me. All these things belonged to a man who thought that my ideas were inadequate for the future that he wanted.

I felt a revulsion and I wanted to desecrate his belongings. I wanted to tear the pages from the book that had been more desirable than I. I thought about throwing his laundry in the garbage can. Terrible thoughts came to me. I felt a violence I had not known before.

My anger got the better of my sorrow. My mind raced crazily. I imagined myself rearranging his razor so that when he shaved he would cut himself. I wondered if I weakened a link in his bicycle chain if it would break when he most depended on it. I could see him critically injured, riding his run-away bicycle into a moving automobile. In my fantasy I killed him because he had killed me. I hated him because I loved him. I wept tears more justifiable for a dead man than for one still alive.

I put aside his belongings and began to "shut down the house," as we called it. When I turned off the front porch light I remembered how tenderly he had kissed me goodbye. There had been tears in his eyes when he looked at me and said, sadly, "I love you."

When I undressed I looked at the queen-size bed and realized that in more than a year, this would be the first time I would sleep alone and I couldn't understand why I was alone.

"I love you," I could hear him saying when he left, like a soldier going off to war to do his duty.

His *duty*! It suddenly hit me. I sat up in bed. That was *it*! For Kevin, marriage was a duty. Something he had to do, been programmed for, all his life.

The clue was in the way he had left, in the way he had held on to me. He wanted to stay, I know that, but morally he had to leave.

"Most men don't *want* to get married," I said to the empty house. "Of all the men in the world, *I* fall in love with a guy who..." My tears flowed and I gave in to them. The long night and my whole life stretched before me in one long continuous ache.

Chapter 4

"Friend"

I had been expecting Catherine's phone call about Kevin's leaving. When he didn't follow through on his promise to go camping with her I saw the beginning of the end. I knew that Catherine had looked forward to that camping trip. And when they didn't go she said it was like a door shutting on their future together.

"Glen," she called out to me one day, "Kevin and I are going up to the mountains this week-end." She could as well have said they were going to the moon, she was that excited.

"That's great, Doll. I'm glad..." She had no ears to hear me. She announced her mood by the way she walked across the law school classroom to our desks, clicking her heels on the vinyl floor, dropping her books on her desk, and flinging her coat over her chair.

"We're leaving right after work, Friday," she beamed, sitting down and mechanically thumbing through her notes. "We're going to stay at the same place we went after we first met. Remember where I told you we went?"

"Yes." I remembered how happy she had been at that time. "Yes," I repeated, nodding my head.

"Kevin's getting our fishing licenses. Our old ones expired. I can hardly wait."

I wanted to tell her then how I felt. I wanted to caution her, "Be careful. Don't get your hopes up. He's not going to do it. You'll wait for him and he won't come home. He does it every time. You'll never *get* to that cabin again."

But I saw the excitement she felt. I loved to see her happy, but my suspicions told me that this was all leading to another disappointment.

"We're going to rent the same cabin," she told me, softening her voice as other students began to fill the classroom. I nodded, smiling to her, wanting my premonitions to be wrong. But they weren't.

I didn't know until the following Tuesday that they hadn't gone on their trip. She told me that Kevin came home late that Friday because he had to prepare papers for his boss. He said he was too tired and that they would drive up to the mountains on Saturday.

"If you're too tired, *I'll* drive tonight," Catherine volunteered.

"I'm too tired to *go* tonight, sweetheart," he said, "no matter *who* drives." So they would wait until the next day.

When the phone rang early Saturday morning, Kevin went to the office to finish some last minute work for his boss. Catherine said she successfully kept her spirits up until the afternoon wore itself down to four o'clock. But when Kevin returned after five o'clock, her anticipation had burned itself out. They decided not to go at all. It was a "waste of time," he told her, offering instead to take her out to dinner and to a movie. At any other time that was an invitation she would have welcomed.

Because I knew how much that trip meant to her, my heart reached out. I wanted to help prepare her for the worst. It seemed to me that their break-up had been inevitable almost from the first.

I remembered the night they had met at a party for one of the law students leaving to finish her degree in another state. It wasn't a party for couples, lots of students were dropping in, even students from other law schools, and that included Kevin. I saw Catherine talking and laughing with a group and I joined them. She introduced me.

"Glen, this is Kevin...What did you say your last name was, Kevin? Oh, never mind. We don't use last names anyway."

We shook hands and I was going to say something to him but he turned from me, though I knew he saw my question forming. His action appeared deliberate and it bothered me. I turned my attention to Catherine.

There is a way that she laughs when she wants to attract a certain man. I recognized that laugh and so I began to study Kevin carefully. They talked and laughed, not really seeing or hearing much of anything else going on around them. It was soon obvious to me that they were caught up in each other, and that bothered me too.

This Kevin had a supercilious air about him, reminiscent of someone else I'd known years ago. I had the distinct feeling in the way he shook my hand, looking away from me in perfect timing to subordinate me, and even in the way he was talking to Catherine, that for this evening he was slumming.

"What *is* your percentage of students

from your school who pass the state bar?"
I heard him ask Catherine. *He* knew that
answer, because all law students know
the percentages.

"It's not as high as the percentage for
your school," Catherine was forced to
answer.

"But for the number of years our
school has existed, our percentage over
the long term is quite high," she said
weakly.

"Yes, well...lately, however...say,
how about some more of that spiked
punch?" Possessively he wheeled her
around, away from me.

Maybe he had been testing me, or
testing Catherine. Maybe he wanted to
see if I was her date. I laughed to myself.
He needn't have bothered, if *that* was his
question. But as my father would have
said, "I didn't like his altitude."

I wasn't worried about his snubbing
me, but I was worried even on that first
night about Catherine. The men she had
been involved with before had all been...
what shall I say?...socially her inferior?
She had seemed to have an "I want to
help you" relationship before, encourag-
ing her past loves to go on to college, or
aspire in their jobs, to make more of

themselves than they were. If this association with Kevin clicked, it would be a new kind of relationship for her. This would be the first man I would have seen her with who considered himself *her* superior. I didn't figure this all out then of course, but gradually I began to see that because this was a new status, so to speak, for Catherine, she would be vulnerable and... unprepared.

As long as she had been the controlling partner in her love affairs she had nothing to lose. Not that she had been unfair. But it was obvious to me that she was not all that interested in the others, in Al for instance. But this affair with Kevin, if that's what it would turn out to be, would be different.

What would happen to her independence? Would a different Catherine emerge? Would that needy part of herself, just as years ago the needy part of myself, come forward and try to claim it due?

At times the wisp of a question had presented itself to me. Was she searching for some assurance? Had she never been assured that she was really okay? She was the picture of a person who had everything going for her. But I suspected at times that in some back room of her personality she might be compensating for an important missing ingredient.

I tried a layman's analysis of her problem. I knew that she had worried about her height, but lately she seemed to feel that being tall was an asset. I knew she came from a good family, whatever that means. Her mother and father were divorced, but even that she spoke of as a positive thing. I'd met her mother last Easter when she flew down to Hollywood for a few days. Immediately she and I got along great. I envied the warm feelings obvious between Catherine and her mother.

I'd never met her father and Catherine never talked about him except one time when I asked. She said he was a very intelligent man and he had retired from an important position with I.B.M. She appeared to brace herself when she spoke of him, set on not letting her guard down. I don't know why I didn't want to pry, because everything else about her was an open book. But I knew there were areas about her that were vulnerable and for reasons I didn't understand, I felt protective of her.

It was less than two months after they met at the law school party that I knew Catherine and Kevin had rented that small cottage and were living together.

"Kevin's a dream," Catherine told me. "I've finally found the right man for me."

I tried to be happy for her, but all my senses told me that Kevin was making a stop-over.

"I'm glad for you, glad you're happy. Kevin's a smart man." That was the best I could do.

"He has really planned out his future," she said. "He hopes to be a judge before he's forty." His ambition, at first, attracted her.

"Are *you* in his plans?" I tried to sound only mildly concerned.

"Of course!"

I wondered about that as the months passed. If I had charted their course by what Catherine told me, or by her moods when we met in our classes, all the lines would have run down hill. I could only believe as time went on that Kevin had not gotten something that he wanted, whatever that was.

"Maybe you're worrying too much," I ventured one evening when we'd gone to a movie. She had called me because Kevin was working all week-end. I could tell by her voice over the phone that she was feeling down. So when I picked her up I had some new jokes and I put my best spirits right out front so she could join in with my repartee. That always worked with her.

Our light-heartedness lasted all through the show and into our fish-and-chips afterwards, and then it dissipated like the air going out of a balloon. I could no longer hold her up and she started to cry. That's when I said she was worrying too much. She shook her head up and down, agreeing with me.

"Sorry about the tears," she said. "I've spent a lot of tears on Kevin."

"Too many," I wanted to say.

"I can't get over how so many things about him hurt me," she cried wiping her eyes carefully to preserve her mascara.

I looked at her, saying many things to myself that I couldn't say to her. Kevin's a formalist, my words would have said. He had been living by himself, determined on his course of action when he met you and you side-tracked him.

Because he's side-tracked, I went on explaining to myself, he's not working as hard on his goals as he had planned, and because of that he feels guilty. And if he feels guilty, then who's he going to blame for that guilt?

I'm sure he feels guilty, also, about living with you, I thought. I'll even bet the guilt at first heightened his excitement about the whole love affair. I've known my own guilt to do that. Guilt is not *all* negative.

"When we go to visit his parents," Catherine interrupted my thinking, moving her empty plate aside, "we sleep in separate bedrooms. He doesn't want his parents to know that we are living together."

"How does that make you feel?"

"Oh, I miss him."

"No. I mean...psychologically?"

"Well, he doesn't want to hurt his mother."

And *you*, I asked myself, what about hurting *you*? Aloud I asked, "And when both of you go to visit *your* mother?"

"We sleep together," she smiled. She was reflective for a moment and then added, "I guess that makes *him* feel guilty. I never thought about that before. Just because I'm at ease, I assumed he would be too. You know," she asked solemnly, "he wants to get married?"

"Yes. You told me."

110

"I think living together makes him feel guilty," she said. "Funny, I thought it was *women* who were meant to feel guilty."

"I guess it all depends on how free each of us has been...or if we've been free to grow up to be ourselves...or...if we've had to grow up to be what our parents want us to be." In saying that I was suddenly filled with all the feelings of worry and guilt of my own childhood.

I'm no psychologist but it seemed when Kevin's guilt feelings were getting too strong for him, that was about the time that Catherine told me he was secretly drinking. "When I came into the kitchen unexpectedly and saw him tipping the whiskey bottle into his mouth, not even making himself a drink in a glass, but drinking right out of the bottle, I was surprised," she told me some time ago.

"But what surprised me more," she had said, "was Kevin's reaction. He was *furious* with me. Accused me of spying on him. He didn't want me to know about that drinking. Or...that's what I felt then, but now, it's strange to say... somehow looking back on it, I felt that he really *did* want me to know about it. I was part of his game. It would be more

111

fun for him if I didn't catch him at it. At the same time...he wanted it to be his own secret. I felt he wanted to play hide-and-seek and have the chance to get angry at me if I caught him."

"And his keeping his sleeping with you a secret from his mother," I asked, "do you think it's the same thing? Do you think that made it more exciting for him...putting something over on some-one. Having a secret guilt?"

"Now you're getting too complicated," she said, off-hand, but I could see she was thinking about that.

I was afraid then, I'd given her some-thing more to worry about. That had not been my intention. I wanted to help her, but the thought of guilt and its destruc-tiveness wouldn't leave me.

I was seldom free of guilt myself, but for me it was a burden. At one time I felt so weighted down by it I thought the only relief would be to commit suicide. In talk-ing to Catherine one day I began to get some relief from that terrible feeling. It was about a year ago, after she had asked me if I'd double-date with Al and her. She said her plan was for me to ask her room-mate, Debbie, to be my date.

"Debbie's nice. You'll like her," she

said when we'd gone to have coffee after one of our classes. Somehow as first year law students, Catherine and I had gravitated toward each other. In the maze of a hundred or so new students, full of anxieties and expectations, our two lives had come together in a few classes and at a couple of parties and we found that we enjoyed being together. She laughed at my jokes and I liked to be funny for her. But when she began pushing too hard about Debbie I knew I had to be honest with her or I would lose her friendship. I might lose her friendship by *being* honest, but I had to risk that.

"Look, Doll," I said, "there's something you've got to know..." I paused, not sure how to say it. I had imagined this conversation many times with many different people, but here, for the first time, I was actually saying this. "I don't go out with girls," I said flatly.

She made no response. I thought that the message hadn't penetrated. Actually it was no surprise to her since I never did date anyone she knew.

"I go out with boys," I said.

She stirred her coffee, looking at me sideways to make sure I was serious because I *did* joke a lot. She clinked her spoon back and forth against the side of her cup. I felt disengaged from everything, waiting.

Finally she said, "You're . . . you're telling me that you're gay? A homosexual?" She stopped stirring her cup and looked at me directly.

"Yes." And there came all that guilt again, just as it did when my mother would want me to take Dottie Kerb to the high school dance.

"It's time you started dating," my mother would laugh nervously, and I would force myself to phone Dottie and go with a group to a show or to a dance even though I had known all along that there was something different with me.

When we would park the car and the other fellows would kiss their girls I would try to get the same response as they did from the girl I was dating but I never felt that I succeeded. I had heard of homosexuals and I was pretty sure that that's what I was, but because they were referred to as "sick" or "perverts," I tried desperately to get myself out of being a homosexual. I believed that if I dated lots of girls and forced myself to have sex with them that I would get over the feelings I had for some of the boys I knew.

Maybe it was because we were all young and inexperienced and the girls I did date didn't know good sex from indifferent sex that I wasn't detected. That should have pleased me, but instead it raised my fears. Before, I had felt terrible because I was some kind of freak, but when I started the deception I felt worse because I knew I was not being fair to the girls. Either way I felt guilty and I didn't know what I was guilty of.

When Mary Samuelson said she thought she was in love with me, I tried very hard to pretend that I was in love with her. I thought it might change me. My parents were happy. They saw that I was normal. Mary's parents thought we were the best looking couple in high school. And as for me, I wondered how long I could pretend feelings I didn't feel, and hold up under what I was doing.

I might have gone on forever, even with marriage and children, if I hadn't met Paul. We were at the high school senior picnic, swimming, playing baseball, eating hot dogs, and getting sunburned. Everybody was preparing to go home when I dove into the lake one more time to cool off.

I went down to the bottom and started to come up, enjoying the long, slow pulls of my arms, when I felt somebody encircle my body. I opened my eyes and saw that I was face to face under water with Paul, the school newspaper editor. We looked at each other, bubbles rising in front of our faces.

He held one arm around my waist while he moved his other hand over my stomach, into my trunks, and tenderly touched my genitals. My body instantly ached with the ecstasy of his touch. If we hadn't surfaced abruptly we would have drowned in each other's arms.

Treading water I stared at him and he smiled. I saw that he wasn't making fun of me.

"How did you know?" I asked.

"I don't know how I knew. I just did."

I wanted to go under water again and nodded with my head to indicate that. "Wait," he said. "We'll be missed. The bus will be leaving."

I felt I had been robbed of what I wanted most.

"I have an idea." He spit water away from us. "My folks will be gone tonight. Why don't you come over. I have to take

Nancy out on a date, but I can be a little late. Come around six-thirty." He swam off toward shore, not waiting for my answer because he already knew it.

Our affair lasted for a year. Even though we both went to different colleges, we met regularly either away from home or at our own homes in our parents' absence. Except for sex we had nothing in common. Paul was an extrovert, winning his way through college on a journalism scholarship. I was an introverted humanities major, taking my parents' money and living from day to day, not really knowing where I was going.

I didn't love Paul. In fact I didn't really like him. He was using me and I knew it. But then, I had to admit, I was using him too. He had ways of making me feel that I was junior to him and I resented that. I think that was one reason why I disliked Kevin. He reminded me of Paul.

It was on Paul that my body was dependent and I couldn't disentangle myself from him. Eventually I began to hate myself for being enslaved to the demands of my body, and especially with someone I didn't like. Yet I was destitute when Paul found someone else. He dropped me flat and I wanted to die. I didn't know what to do until I learned to find the places where I could meet other men who were like me and we would sneak a few hours a week to be ourselves...someplace in hiding to avoid the violence that "straight" men were known to inflict on men like us. It was risky, but one thing was sure—after that afternoon at the high school picnic, I would just have to take my chance, guilt and fear and all, because I knew I couldn't exist ever again for very long without having sex with another man.

"Don't you like having sex with women?" Catherine asked that day in the coffee shop.

"There is no comparison for me with having sex with a man."

"Have you always been a..."

"Queer?"

"No. I didn't say that.... Have you always been a homosexual?" I felt compassion for Catherine. She had just learned that her good friend was not "normal."

"Yes," I answered, "I have always been. I don't think anything happened that *changed* me from heterosexual to homosexual. I think it was the way I was born."

"But how can that be? I thought all

homosexuals had ... authoritative fathers, or absent fathers, or something like that ... over-indulgent mothers. Things like that. I thought there was some ... conditioning ... when kids were little."

"I've read all the theories, too, Catherine, believe me! I don't fit any of the theories. I suppose maybe some people do. But I've never known any who did."

"I never thought much about it before." She began to sip her coffee.

"No. There would be no need for you to."

"But now that I know that one of my best friends is a ..." I thought she was going to have difficulty saying it. It reminded me of what I'd heard about Alcoholics Anonymous. If you can admit it, you can face up to it. "Homosexual," she said and smiled at me. "I better learn to understand it."

"There's nothing to understand, Catherine."

"Why are you calling me 'Catherine'?"

"I'm sorry ... I think I felt ... well, sort of estranged. The information I just gave you might have spoiled our friendship and I didn't want to ..."

"Be too friendly?"

"Yes ... that could be it."

"Please don't call me 'Catherine.' I feel I've lost something when you do that."

"Okay, Doll," I said and we smiled together, both looking over our coffee cups into each other's eyes, nothing between us. I had taken a big risk and hadn't lost anything. In fact I had gained many things I needed. She put her hand over mine. I had never had such a good free feeling. For the first time that I could remember I felt soul clean.

From then on, her happiness was even more of a concern of mine. I could have loved her, which of course I did, though not in a romantic sense.

When her phone call came about Kevin and I heard her crying I almost cried with her, but I knew that would be no help.

I saw her the next night at school. She was rigid, but surviving. I squeezed her arm when she sat next to me and I looked at her to tell her with my eyes that I was with her. She smiled through lips she was biting, but the tears did not fall.

After class I walked with her to her car and then as we agreed, I followed her home. Driving, I wondered about what I would say to help her. I thought I would probably repeat everything I'd already said. I couldn't think of anything new. Well, anyway I'd stay for awhile and that might help.

She arrived home a few minutes before me and stood waiting for me at the door. She was trying to smile and that made me happy.

"Hi, Doll. How about putting on some records?"

"Sure. On low."

We shuffled through some favorites and I selected a couple.

"No. They're too sad," she said. She selected different ones. I felt she was on the mend. Or at least not torturing herself. I was encouraged.

We disco-danced to the music, each of us a million miles away from the other.

"My mother's coming tomorrow," she said.

"Good!"

"And I talked to my dad. That wasn't so hot, but I'll maybe try to talk to him again." I didn't have any opinion on that, but I saw that she was trying to help herself.

"And someday," she said, "when I understand myself better, I'm going to find the *real* right man." She smiled a half smile that made a joke on herself and waited to see that I recognized it. We laughed together.

"The *real* right man," I repeated, and then I said, "What's wrong with *me*?"

It was as if someone else had said it. I was surprised and instantly sorry. Not because I didn't mean it. Every emotional part of me responded to what I had unexpectedly said. I didn't understand it. But it was more than she should have to deal with right now.

"Oh, I'm sorry," I said. We had both stopped dancing and she stood looking away, unsmiling.

I had ruined something and I needed to rescue the moment. The music beat on and I moved my feet to its rhythm again. Trying nonchalantly I said, "You know *me*, Doll. I don't date girls."

She smiled and I knew we were okay again.

Chapter 5

"Lover"

The most difficult thing I ever did in my life was to turn back and walk down the stairs from Catherine. I was finally acting on my decision that I would no longer live with her. And with the passing of time, and with determination I would no longer love her.

In the small Hollywood home we had shared as lovers for the past year, I was leaving behind not only my lovely Catherine, but also the man I had tried to become. Because I loved her, I had wanted to change, as Catherine would say, "to be free," and I had made efforts to "enjoy and relax more," without feeling guilty.

And though in the first warm energy of our love I felt that I was changing "loosening up," as she would say, I found that after some months had passed and the euphoria began to fade, I often felt tense. I even had a revulsion for what I had been doing. I saw myself as a phoney play-actor living out the life style of someone else's life, and I disapproved of the man I saw on stage. Catherine could sense those moments. She would know something was wrong and at first she could change my moods.

She would come home on a Friday night, for instance, with her bubbling enthusiasm for some week-end activity, she'd talk about the unpolluted air, or the clear weather predictions, and I would find myself caught up in her high spirits. After haphazard preparations we would be packing her ten-year-old camper and driving up into the mountains to spend two days in the snow, when all the week before I had been planning to spend at least Saturday in the law office.

But once we were in the mountains, in our childish games, throwing snow balls or building snow families, I would be too happy to worry about not working, and I did relax and have fun. I can smile now when I think of the time when snow from the branches overhead melted from the heat of our Coleman stove and dropped in blobs, snuffing out the flames. We laughed at our own stupidity, but nonplussed we simply changed our plans and decided to make love instead of making dinner.

She could change like that from whatever she planned, to something else. And in the first months I admired this in her, as I understand we admire in others the things we lack in ourselves. I loved her ability to shift. I called it her sense of adventure into new territories. We did things neither one of us had done before. She even had me cooking mushrooms, and before I met her I had never cooked anything.

There were times when we got out of bed while it was still dark and we'd jog down to the beach to watch the sun rise. We sat in the cold, wet sand and shivered in our own private sun worship and we loved it and each other. We did many new things together. We were sure that we even invented new ways to make love that nobody in the whole history of humanity had ever tried before.

I guess love made it all exciting. And because our love was new there was an unreal quality about our life together, like the suspension of reality when you walk through Disneyland. I remember those first Sunday mornings when we shared the newspaper. It was like a love ritual passing the sections back and forth. I suppose that if all those feelings could have held strong, the other feelings I had, the feelings that began to sink in, of not liking the way I was living, those feelings would never have had a chance to take hold.

But after I began to see that there was no future in my love for Catherine, when I knew for sure she really didn't want to get married, I no longer enjoyed doing most of the things that had given me a high only months before. And yet I continued to love her.

The night I walked down those stairs away from her, after we had argued and she had told me I might as well leave, I held her in my arms and she started to cry. "But you *love* me, Kevin. We don't need to break up. And *I* love you. I've never loved anyone as much as I love you. Please! Please, let's try to make it work."

"It won't work, Catherine." I had thought this through. "You have different ideas, different... It's best this way, before we get more involved."

"More involved? How could I get *more* involved? My life revolves around you. You're what makes me happy—or unhappy. You're..." Then she started crying again and she couldn't speak.

I wanted to ease the terrible feelings of loneliness she was having because I was having those feelings too. To be separate now when we'd been together for a year was frightening, but we'd have to do it. We'd have to be strong to face the emptiness ahead of us. I knew it would be lonely for both of us. I had been lonely ever since I had decided to leave, many months ago when I first felt that hollowness. That was when I learned Catherine's opinion about marriage, and about children.

"Would it go *on* like this?" I had asked her then. We were standing in the bedroom, getting ready to go to bed. I had said something about when we were married. It was a conversation we'd had casually once, but I hadn't felt she was serious before. She looked at me after I asked my question and then she stepped out of her long-legged denims, dropped them in the dirty clothes corner of the room and said once more that she didn't really want to get married.

"But to *me*," I said. "You do...you will want to marry me? After I pass the bar and..."

"My darling," she said kindly, "I don't want to marry anyone...at anytime. What's the point? We don't need to get married." She took off her bikini underwear and stood in front of me in the nude. "I love you," she said and smiled. I turned away from her, not to be distracted. She put her robe over her shoulders and sat down on the edge of the bed. "What more is it that you want?" she asked simply.

I couldn't find my words. I understood the meaning of her question. We had each other and that was enough for her. Why wasn't it enough for me? I turned to her and admired her naked beauty.

"I love you," I told her.

"Then come here, will you?" I postponed my concern.

On that night there were no answers to her question, "What more is it that you want?" because as on all nights her body and my love for her made any interest in the future irrelevant.

But daylight brought the answers that eluded me in the night. "What more was it that I wanted?" I asked myself. That was the question Catherine had asked.

"Respectability," I told myself, driving to work the next day. "I feel I'm being furtive. That's okay for awhile—even exciting—but it's not okay for a lifetime. It lacks a quality...respectability.

"What do you care what others think?" Catherine had asked.

"It's important. I'm not going to get the positions I want, the promotions I want, if the partners in a law firm look at my private life and see me as someone who's living with a woman—and I don't *care* how many other thousands of couples are living like this. To me it *matters*."

"If you're not promoted because of your life-style, well, that's illegal."

"So what! What's legal is one thing. What people do is another. You and your 'liberation.'"

I knew I had touched a sensitive part of her so I tried to tone it down.

"Look sweetheart, ideals are fine, and sure we should all be able to live the way we want and not have it affect our jobs. But that's the ideal. The truth is, the way we live does affect whether we are hired or promoted. A wife is a social asset to any company, but a live-in girl friend is something else."

"God, you make it sound almost dirty."

"I'm sorry. I don't mean to do that."

"If we can't live the way we want, not twisting and turning to fit what society wants, then what *are* we?"

"Cath, I know how you feel. I've gone over all of this in my mind a hundred times. But the truth is, even in spite of what I feel about promotions and all that, I really don't want...I want us to get married. As a permanent arrangement."

Remnants of last night's conversation persisted until I reached downtown Hollywood. "Respectability," I told myself, "means a wife and a family. At least to me it does. I don't want a childless love nest. I want a noisy family with children who will grow up together as my sisters and my brother and I did.

"It's empty," I said out loud, driving my VW Bug into the parking lot next to the law offices. "It's great when we're making love, but...it has no future." I parked my car and pocketed the keys.

"Have I been kidding myself? Shouldn't I have expected that all this would lead to getting married? And after that, to children?"

All my childhood pictures of what life

would be as an adult were pictures of me with a family. I had always seen myself living in a conventional house—even a house in a row. My wife greeted me when I came home and our children ran to meet me. I picked them up and held them. They were happy pictures, full of the action and noises of a large family. Where would I be without that?

What would I be?

I pushed the revolving doors of the office building and walked through the foyer, punched the elevator button more times than it needed and decided that I'd stop by and see Steve on my way home when the day was over.

It must have been the conversation last night that triggered all the reminiscences of my life with my father and mother when all of us kids were home, running in and out of the house, teasing mom if she started to get crabby, playing games on each other.

There were times after I grew up when I ached for that childhood with my family, and it seemed I needed to see at least some of them periodically to talk about old times, to laugh together, and even to cry together when we remembered sad times—especially when we talked about that time our favorite old dog was poisoned.

We were glad we came from a large family because we'd always have someone to share our childhood memories. It was the kind of growing up I wanted for *my* children. It wasn't all fun of course. We had our problems like everyone else in those times.

We weren't much different than the other families in our neighborhood. We all had trouble over money because there was never enough. But in my family we were advised, "Do your homework, do well in school, and you'll get a good job and you'll make good money."

"And if I go to college?" I remember asking my father one day.

It was an unexpected question. No one in my parents' families had ever gone to college. "You're on your own," my father answered.

I felt deserted.

"We don't have money for you kids to go to college," he said. "You ought to know that, Kevin. You get through high school and find a job. At least there *are* jobs for you when you graduate. When *I* graduated from high school..." That's where I drifted off because I'd heard it all before. I came back to the conversation when he was saying, "...anything I got out of life I earned myself."

I know, Dad, I said to myself, when you graduated from high school in the middle of the depression, there were no jobs. But you made it. And now you're up to minimum wage. No thanks! I'm not going to end up on any factory assembly line!

"I'm going to college," I announced. I had thought of it for a long time. Now, here I was, talking about it. "I'll go to the junior college. That doesn't cost anything."

"You'll be living at home. *That* cost something."

"But, Dad...I'm your *son*! Surely I can live at home."

"Yes...yes..." he relented. "If you're set on this. Don't see that it will do much good though. But if you do, you know I have to be fair to the four of you. If I give to one...if I let you stay here without contributing after you graduate from high school...when I was your age as soon as I graduated from high school I was expected to contribute to the household."

"I know. You've told us. And I know

you have to give to all of us equally. But, Dad, maybe the others won't *want* to go to college."

"You, Kevin, you'll give them the idea, and then they'll want to go." He made it sound like I might give them a disease.

That's when my mom came into the room. She was the one who pushed education. She was the leader in our family. She was the one who read us books when we were young, who was always trying to get us to turn off the T.V. and to read something "worthwhile." She was the one who brooded during the long weekends when "her men" watched football all day long and then watched all the reruns in the evening.

"What a waste," she would mumble just loud enough so I could hear, but never loud enough for Dad.

"Did I hear something about college?" she asked.

"Kevin here, says he's gonna go to the junior college. I mean in two years... when he graduates from high school," my dad almost scoffed.

"I'm pleased about that, son," my mother told me. "And from the junior college... you can go on. I know you will.

And..." Her mind wandered. "I wish *I* could have gone to college," she said wistfully. "But I'll do all I can to help *you*.

She kissed the top of my head. She had long ago given up hugging me like she used to. My dad told her that hugging her boys would make sissies of his sons. I saw my father look at her, tilting his head the way he did when he was about to ask a question.

"When you get finished with our two-year college here," my mother said all in a rush as though to get it out now that this moment had arrived, "and you're ready to go on to the university, maybe I can get a job to help out on the money."

"No." My father was firm. "Mother, you have a full-time job right here. *My* wife is not going to work."

My mother didn't say anything. She stood silently, looking at me. My father continued. "There's three more, younger'n Kevin, and they need you at home. Kids'll go bad if they don't have a mother at home."

Still my mother did not say anything, but then I had never heard her contradict my father.

"A man," my father said, "who lets his wife work, isn't much of a man."

My mother had no words. I was glad then that she hadn't said anything because I didn't want her to get scolded by my dad. And I didn't want to be the cause of my brother or sisters getting into trouble just because nobody was at home to take care of them. Nor did I want any part of making my dad feel that he wasn't in charge of his family.

"My family is my first responsibility," he had often told us, and we appreciated that. "I never made much money," he admitted, "but all of the money I *did* make has gone into giving you kids a solid family life."

We would nod our appreciation.

"I've lived my life for mother and you kids," he'd announce periodically. My mother would smile her grateful smile. "I never gamble," he boasted, "never ran after women. Never boozed it up."

Though I realized that there were things about my father I didn't like, that is, things like his never reading anything, and never having any facts, yet always being an authority on any subject, I still respected him as the head of our family. Sometimes as I grew up I was embarrassed about him when I knew he was speaking about things he really didn't know anything about. Yet I admired him for his other qualities.

"That's true, Frank," his friends from the plant would agree when they stopped by the house and he would talk to them about welfare people robbing the government, and politicians mismanaging federal funds, and Spicks and Niggers having natural inferiority. When I was younger I was proud that my father knew so much, but when I grew older I began to see holes in his statements. That was one reason why I wanted to have facts and why I set high goals for myself in school.

I learned just about everything I could get my hands on. I couldn't trust not knowing something. I was going to get someplace in this world and I knew I couldn't get there by bluffing. But while I didn't agree with my father about lots of things he said, I never argued with him, and I certainly didn't question his right to tell my mother to stay home.

We had all seen other mothers in our neighborhood get jobs. We knew when the kids in the families came home from school, nobody was home. "What good is the working?" my dad asked.

"They have a freezer and two cars," my brother reminded him.

"Yes. They do," my father agreed. "But the second car is so the wife can work. Think of the money it costs for her clothes, so she *can* work. It cost more money for a wife to work than if she stayed with her family where she belongs." I couldn't disagree because I didn't know the statistics.

As other mothers in our neighborhood found jobs, we bragged about *our* mother not working. It made us feel superior to the others. Anyway, she was so busy at home I wondered how she could possibly have done everything and gone to work too.

I managed the cost of my education without their help. With student loans and then after my stint in the army that entitled me to veteran's benefits, I finished at the university and now I was even finishing law school. And when I was all through I calculated I would have about five thousand dollars to pay back to Uncle Sam for the student loans. I explained my figures to Catherine one time when we were projecting our future together. I told her I'd be clear financially in about three years, even with a wife and children to support. That was the night she told me she didn't want to have any children. It had never occurred to me to not have children.

"But you'll be my *wife*..." I was dismayed. "And we'll have a family, and..."

"Kevin," she stopped me, "you create beautiful pictures for yourself with me in them, but you don't ask *me*."

"Well...I just assumed."

"Yes...that's just it. You assumed."

That was the first time we had a conversation about the years ahead. I had had no inkling before, that her ideas would be different than mine. I couldn't believe she didn't want children. That seemed...unnatural. *All* women wanted marriage and children. I never thought *any* woman, really, didn't want children. It was what people looked forward to. But Catherine said children would prevent her from living her life. It would be, she said, that *her* life would be over and from then on it would be the childrens' lives that would dominate. She didn't want that kind of a life. That was a surprise to me.

Wasn't having children a woman's life?

Why was she so different from other women?

Had Catherine been too...hurt by

her parents' divorce? I could think of several of my friends whose parents had divorced. And the kids went on and got married and *they* had kids. I couldn't understand Catherine's thinking. That's why Steve was good for me to talk to. It's good to listen to yourself talk to a friend. That way I could hear my ideas and see how they sounded. It's a good way, I told him, to test my ideas.

"It's not *you* who should be testing your ideas," he said to me. "It's *Catherine* who should hear herself talk."

I liked talking with Steve. He was one of my oldest friends, from the old neighborhood in Fresno. One of the childhood friends I hadn't lost touch with. He and I had been altar boys when we were young. That was when my mother was hopeful that I'd become a priest.

Steve and I started out in junior college together but his grades were so low he finally quit before he was put on probation. He always had money though, when I never had more than enough to scrape through. He worked in light constuction during the building boom of the late 50's, and eventually got on as an apprentice plumber. We never lost track of each other and once when I was really stuck for money, while I was waiting for a lost G.I. check, Steve loaned me three hundred dollars.

"What's a buddy for?" he asked, smiling his big, broad grin. "Someday after you're a lawyer, I'll come to you for three hundred dollars worth of legal advice." I think it somehow made up for the embarrassment he felt when he received those low grades.

Steve and his wife lived comfortably now in one of the units of the triplex apartment house they had bought. They were frugal, though as Steve said, they would have a lot more money in the bank if Sandy went to work.

"She has a degree in accounting, you know." He was proud of that. "It helps in our bookkeeping here. She could get a job with any C.P.A., but we agreed together that her life here with me and little Tommy is more important that any job."

I envied Steve the set pattern of his life.

I knew all the things that Steve would say before he even said them, but I guess I needed to hear them. If I hadn't needed some reinforcement for my point of view I would have gone straight home from work. At Steve's I felt "at home," comfortable—again.

"Your ideas are age-old, well established," he said. "*Your* ideas don't need testing. It's natural for men and women to want to get married and have children. You're on the side of the angels, friend. It's *Catherine* who's...twisted."

I didn't like him saying that. I knew he disapproved of Catherine, but still I didn't want him to say things like that.

"She has," he went on, "Oh, I don't know what to call it...she's been too liberated. She's so liberated she isn't anywhere. She's floating...."

I could agree with that. I had thought something like that about Catherine myself, though I'd not used those words. She moved so easily from one thing to another. Oh...not flighty...but it didn't bother her to change her plans. I had once admired her for that. Now, I didn't know. She'd decide to do something, and off we'd go. She often said she liked people with a "let's personality."

"What's that mean?" I had asked her. That was when we first met and we were doing all those new things together.

"Well I just said, 'Let's go to the new

exhibit at the Museum of Modern Art,' and you said, 'Yes.' Not long ago *you* said, 'Let's ride our bikes down to the corner and get a pizza,' and I said, 'Yes....' See what I mean? We both have a 'Let's personality.'''

But Steve had used the word "floating." I wondered if that were the same thing. I didn't think so.

"She's not sure what she's doing," Steve said.

"She's finishing law school, and working for the same judge for two years as a law clerk."

"Yes, but I mean, she doesn't know where she's going. Look at how she happened to get into law school."

"She applied and got accepted. What do you mean?"

"I mean, it's not like people usually go to law school. I remember you made up your mind in the last year of high school. I remember that you were determined a long time ago. You set your goals and headed right for them. But Catherine, remember the night she was telling us how she decided to go to law school?"

I remembered. I thought it was extraordinary at the time.

"No teaching jobs," Steve said. "She graduated from college to be a teacher and there were no teaching jobs so she got a job as a legal secretary."

"Which she never started," I said. I had admired her when she had told us about those decisions. I could see Steve's point, but I could also see Catherine's. That made it difficult.

"I know she never started that job," Steve said. "She didn't even follow through on *that*. Her mother tells her, 'why be the secretary, who not be the legal?' and the next thing she's in law school."

"And doing very well." I was proud of her.

"Yes. But don't you see what I'm saying? She blows with the wind." I had to admit that Catherine did change her goals easily. She *could* rearrange her whole life without too much disturbance. That's what troubled me. She wasn't set, like Steve's wife. I could never have made the changes that Catherine made. What troubled me more was that I was sure she would make more changes in her goals and I didn't know where that would leave me.

"We were talking about careers in

law the other night," I admitted to Steve. "And she said, even if she passed the state bar exam next spring, that...that didn't necessarily mean she would practice law."

That had set me back. She'd go through all that, and then possibly not go into the law. If *I* couldn't be a lawyer... after all my years of preparation...well, I don't know, I couldn't see my life any other way.

"See?" Steve asked. "Isn't that what I'm talking about? She floats. You can't pin her down. She's too liberated!"

"I love her."

"Then why do you look at the floor when you say that? Do you regret that you love her?'

His question puzzled me.

"Do you?" he persisted.

"I don't know. I'm confused. I've been trying to figure out this situation for months now and it's...it's wearing me down. I get so uptight trying to work it out, even taking a drink doesn't help me anymore. And then Catherine gets on me about drinking, and that puts more pressure on me. Sometimes I feel, I feel I want to go out and smash all the windows." I stopped because I realized I was going to cry and I had to hold myself in. I'd not think of anything for a minute.

Steve broke the silence. "I can understand why you're tense. You're living one way and you, well, it goes against the grain to try to be what you're not. I remember how you were brought up because my family was like yours. That's why we never took those drug trips like our friends did. Remember what we thought about freaking out? Everybody rushed in to save those kids. What the hell! They brought it on themselves."

What did all this have to do with Catherine and me?

"All that free living, that's when it started. The pill. All that. Remember how you and I felt about that? They were going to hell."

"Yes." I remembered all those things and they had scared me. I saw what I didn't want to become, a zombie, long-haired, no direction, spaced-out. Watching things happen to some of the kids in high school and later in college made me determined. I would not get lost along the way. I owed more than that to my father and to myself.

It was only recently I had been worried about myself. All the tense feelings I had lately. And I *knew* I was drinking too much. But it was all this problem of trying to resolve the situation with Catherine. It was hurting my confidence in myself. Somehow I had gotten off the track.

"It's tied with the future," I said.

"What is?" Steve asked.

"Well..." I searched, not bothering to fill him in on where my mind had wandered. "I love her. I don't know why. Love is...not something I can explain. You asked me if I regret loving Catherine. I would not regret loving her if I saw things in the years ahead more clearly, or, that what I saw was something I wanted to see. I would not regret loving her if...everything were going to go okay."

"But of course not," Steve said, picking up the threads of my thoughts. "When Sandy and I are getting along, which, thank God, is most of the time, I'm very glad that I love her. But when she does some of her stupid things...you know how she forgets things...and, well, like driving the car, how she gets in so many bad jams, honestly, Kevin, at those times I wish I *didn't* love her. I'm almost," he confessed, "ashamed that I love her. Like I wonder how could I love someone so stupid? Or, how do people see *me* being in love with someone who does such dumb things."

I thought about that. How did people see *me*, being in love with Catherine? How did my parents, for instance, see me, their son, in love with the girl I had brought home. And how did they see her? I recalled what my father said about her when we were alone.

"She's too tall."

"Too tall! She's not as tall as *I* am. She's not too tall for *me*."

"I don't like standing next to her."

I hardly ever thought of Catherine's height, but when my father said that, I tried to see her through his eyes. When I first met Catherine at a law school party I was attracted to her because she was outstanding. People looked at her and I liked that. Any woman who is slightly over six feet tall is bound to be noticed.

Then I recalled standing in a group with her later and I realized that I felt intimidated. That's what my father must have meant. I remember thinking, "a woman has no right to be that tall."

My mother had an even more difficult time of it when *she* saw Catherine. I guess I should have prepared my parents better, but that had not occurred to me. All I said over the phone was that I was bringing home the girl I hoped to marry.

"Oh that's nice, Kevin," my mother said. "I'm glad you've finally gotten over Joan."

I wanted to tell her that *I* was the one who broke off those wedding plans with Joan, and I didn't need to "get over" her. But since Mother had taken Joan under her wing and had looked forward to our wedding in the church I didn't think I would mention that point on the eve of bringing Catherine home. I wanted my family to like Catherine.

"You'll like her," I told my mother over the phone, hoping that saying it would make it true.

"Is she Catholic?" my mother asked.

That did it! I knew then that Catherine would have a hard time winning over my mother.

"No, Mother," I had to admit. "She's not Catholic. She's not anything...religious."

My parents were indifferent to her during the visit, but Catherine was her sweetest when we were at their house. She created conversation with my mom, helped Dad pull some weeds and helped with dinner and cleared the table. I think if she'd been Catholic my mother would have warmed up to her and my father might have forgiven her her height.

When it was time for bed at my parents' home, Catherine and I played our game. After elaborately saying our goodnights so that my father and mother could hear us, she went to one bedroom and I went to another. Then when the house was quiet, and I'd heard Dad lock the front door, his last act of each day, I sneaked into Catherine's room.

The excitement of getting away with something, combined with the thrill of our touching nude in the dark, sent my desire for her soaring. It was all I could do to keep from crying out loud with the joy. And try as I did at any other time or any other place, it was impossible to recapture that thrill.

Catherine didn't like our bedtime game at my parents' house. "It's a deception," she said, not smiling. "But if you have to do it, I'll go along with it."

Had my parents known what we were doing they would have more than disapproved. If they knew, too, that when we left their house in Fresno and drove the two hundred miles back to Hollywood, that we were driving to the home we shared together, they would have referred to Catherine as a whore. I'd heard them do that about one of my sister's friends. She was living with her boyfriend as a lot of women were these days, and she made no secret about it.

I never understood how Catherine's mother could let us sleep in the same room together when we went to visit *her*. I lost respect for her when she told us, "Your room is ready." That pointed up to me a major difference in our parents' values.

I think that what Steve called Catherine's liberation must have come from the way things changed in her home when her parents were divorced.

"My mother even told my sister and me she'd give permission for us to have the pill." Catherine was talking about the things that happened after the divorce. "That was years ago, before girls could get the pill on their own...

"Weren't you embarrassed?" I asked.

"We were disgusted," she laughed.

"Did you have boyfriends then? How old were you?"

151

"Sure we had boyfriends, but nothing sexual. Let's see...How old *were* we? That must have been about a year after the divorce. I was, I think I was seventeen, so, Anne was sixteen. The three of us were sitting in the kitchen, talking about Mom's boyfriend?"

"Didn't take her long to get a man. Right?"

"Wrong," Catherine answered coldly. "She didn't go out with anyone for more than a year after the divorce. We assumed she'd be a single woman from then on. But one night she brought home this creep."

"Creep?" I laughed. "You mean your stepfather?"

"No. She didn't marry this guy, thank God. She knew him about...about a year I think. We hated him. Maybe because he was the only man we'd seen with our mother other than our father. Anyway, that night after he left, the three of us are talking together and she calmly announces she's been sleeping with that creep. That wasn't bad enough, but she had to go into a discussion about when we start to have sex she advised us to use birth control pills. Anne and I couldn't believe this was our mother telling us this."

"Didn't she tell you *not* to have sex?" I asked.

"No." Catherine paused. "She must have known we would. Even though we protested that we didn't want to hear about birth control pills, she must have known some day we'd be ready for them."

"She was very...open," I thought aloud. "I'm sure *my* mother never had any kind of conversation like that with my sisters."

"Mmmm...she hadn't always been... that free to talk. It was the divorce. It, it sort of freed us all in a way."

"Sexually, you mean?"

"Oh God, no! I don't mean we all began having sex, sex, sex. I mean we... looked at things differently. Well, I guess you could say we re-evaluated things. And the Creep helped."

"How? If you didn't like him?"

"He was a different kind of person than we'd ever known before. He'd been through some kind of sensitivity training at Esalen. We'd never even heard of that before. He talked about everything and anything, at first embarrassing us terribly. But pretty soon Mom and Anne and I found that we could talk about things together that we'd always felt were forbidden subjects."

"I suppose that was good."

"I think so," she said. "In most families the parents and the kids don't talk much to each other except about unimportant things. At least that was the way it was at our house before the divorce. And the way it *still* is with my dad. He can't seem to talk about anything that matters to any of us personally."

"I have a hard time understanding, though, how your mother could urge you to use the pill."

"Urge! She didn't urge us. She was giving us advice."

"But it disgusted you."

"Then! Way back then! We were young. We were repulsed. But, as it turned out...she was right. She opened the subject up so Anne and I could talk about it together and about a year later we *did* start using the pill."

I thought about that and then asked, "Did your friends know—your girl friends?"

"Sure. A few friends knew. What's the big deal if they knew or not? I'll tell you the difference, though, something Anne noticed too. Our girl friends who were on the pill had to *sneak* to get it, and they felt guilty as hell. One thing for sure, neither Anne nor I *ever* had to take that guilt trip, either about getting the pill, or having sex with our boyfriends."

I found that difficult to believe. "Your mother actually *approved*?"

"She said that our sex life was our own private business and she counted on us to use good judgment." She waited a minute and then went on. "And so," she smiled directly at me for the first time since this conversation started, "I've always used good judgment, wouldn't you say so?"

I knew she was enticing me to be affectionate, but the subject of her past sex life with the freedom she'd had turned my affection off.

"I wonder," I said, "what you'd be like if your mother and father were still living together."

"I don't know. I only know that it was terrible...that divorce." Her mood changed. I reached out to put my hand on her arm.

"But it was a good thing," she said. "All three of us, my mom, Anne, and I, we all...we're such different people than before. We're more broadminded...more tolerant."

"But you said it was terrible!"

"It *was*! We suffered. We cried. Sometimes together. Sometimes by ourselves. But we survived. It was kind of a growth we went through. We had lived in a, well, in a rut you could say. We lived everyday expecting life to go on as usual and then suddenly unbeknownst to anyone beforehand, Mom makes the big decision to leave my dad and we're all...all thrown into a brand new situation. *Everything* is new. We no longer live in a beautiful home. We live in a dinky little apartment. We're no longer part of a...a prestigious family. We're fragments of something that *had* been." She paused.

"From then on," she said, "it was all uphill. I was no longer who I had been. That was hard. I never knew before that the house we lived in and my father's important position all made *me* important to other people. Then...I was nobody. I was like a fish being picked up and dropped in a new pond. Nothing would ever be the same. Our family life was broken. Christmas mornings were gone. All those things gone.

"Oh sure, after a long time, the pain— it leveled off. I got used to change, and then there'd be more changes and I knew we'd never have that old security again. I think that what I learned most about the divorce was that there *isn't* any real security. Anne thinks that her marriage is security. But look at the divorce rate! I *hope* she will be okay, but there is no guarantee for anybody. The future is undependable. You can't count on it."

But *I* do, I said to myself. All that I could find to say was, "It sounds like it was a rough trip."

"Yes, but I'm glad about it now that it happened."

"Glad? You don't sound glad. You're not saying the divorce was good? Not after all that!"

"I think that what I'm saying is that it was what my mother referred to as 'a necessary evil,' and I'm beginning to agree." She thought about that for awhile. "I told my mom, years later, I was proud of her."

"Even after everything she put you through?"

"It took years for me to know what kind of strength she had, to change her life after all those years."

"I see. So it's your mother who taught you to be changeable."

"Kevin, I don't like the way you say that."

"You must admit you change your plans pretty damn often."

"Wait a minute! I don't change just for some...some whimsy. I...Oh...you make me angry. And about my mother... she'd been married for more than twenty-five years. Is *that* changeable? And even if it *is*, she had guts!"

"But you do have to admit..."

"I don't have to admit anything. You make me angry, and...I'm angry at myself for letting you make me angry."

"Ah-hah, I see I've touched a nerve, my sweet."

"Don't get sarcastic like my father."

"Why do you see your father in me. When I take a drink you see your father. When I try to point out something to you, you see your father."

"Sometimes you are like him."

"Just the bad parts, my love?"

"Quit being sarcastic."

"Who's sarcastic?"

"*You* are," she shouted. "If you really wanted to go into this you wouldn't add, 'my love,' in that tone of voice. I recognize it. I heard that tone of voice all my life. It's not a question. It's a slap in the face." She began to cry in a rage, not in sadness, and I didn't pursue that subject. But as long as we were miserable I thought I might as well get all the misery out in the open at one time. I brought up the subject of Glen. I said I wished she'd not call him up when I was working and make those dates with him.

"Why? You have nothing to worry about," she said, her crying stopping abruptly. "Glen is a homosexual."

Was she teasing me? Getting even? No. She explained that it was true. He had told her himself.

I was shocked.

"When did he tell you?" I asked.

"Last spring?"

"He told you last spring and you never told *me*?"

"There's nothing to get so mad about. What was there to tell? What's... I don't see..."

"Don't you think I should know?"

"Why? Sure." She shrugged. "If you want to. I would have told you if I thought you'd wanted..."

"Catherine! Here I am, I see Glen at school.... Sometimes we go out for coffee together."

"Yes. I know you're not great friends, but I'm glad you get along."

"No! For Christ sake! You don't understand. I'm a *man*."

"Wait a minute...."

"People will think I'm..."

"Oh, Kevin," she laughed, the tears hardly dry on her cheeks. Her laugh made me angry. "You think people will think you're..."

"Queer! Can't you see? Why didn't you tell me?"

She became quiet, looking at me, unsmiling.

"The reason you wanted me to tell you was so you...so..." Now *she* was getting angry again. "So you could *avoid* him?"

"Yes. I don't think you were fair with me. Can't you see? It's a reflection on me. People talk! I don't think you should be such pals with him either, going to the movies..."

"Why not?" she asked. "Nothing to fear...right?"

She switched to one of her imperious moods. I'd wait and talk to her again about this when she wasn't emotional. Later I would try to get her to see that her association with Glen was not good. If Glen had told *her* about being a queer, then other people must know. I didn't want us to seem strange. And learning about Glen made me feel strange.

"Glen is my friend," Catherine said. "Whether he is straight or gay has nothing to do with my friendship with him."

I should have been glad I didn't have to worry about his having sex with Catherine, but I didn't think much about that because I was disgusted that we had been associating with a man who would choose to have sex with men.

She knew my feelings but she continued to see Glen, calling him on Saturdays or Sundays when I had to work. It got to be one more thing that bothered me and that's why I mentioned it to Steve on another night when I stopped on my way home from work.

Steve hit the ceiling! He discussed the sin of homosexuality, he explained the Biblical objection, and after he condemned Glen he switched to Catherine, talking about "all her damn freedom." He was very angry.

"It's women like her who... they tear

down important values. It's the damn pill! That's where it started."

"The pill?" I laughed. I couldn't see the connection.

"The pill has value for me too," I told him.

"Yes. I know. Used with common sense," and then he added, not looking at me, "by married couples."

"Oh come on now, Steve...you don't believe...."

"Look what it's done," he said. "All the teenagers in the country have a license to be promiscuous. No morals anymore. Then they bring down the institution of marriage because they're used to being laid by anyone they please. One of the things that used to keep a marriage close together was children, but freedom-loving women say they don't want children 'to tie them down.' They work. Their silly little jobs are more important than their homes.... And they even cavort with homosexuals."

I thought he was carrying this too far. I wanted to put the brakes on him.

"I wonder," I said, "where all of this leaves me."

Steve stopped to think about that.

"I love Catherine," I said. "I love her.

Even after this thing about Glen, I always come back to saying, 'I love her.'"

What were the things about her that I loved, I asked myself. How she smiled when I came home at night, always affectionate. I'd drop my brief case, put my arms around her and we'd stand close to each other for a long time. Catherine said when we did that, we were making up for the absence of the day, the vacancy we felt without each other. She said we needed to get a sense of the other into the sense of ourselves so we could feel whole again. I wouldn't go that far, but I know as soon as I saw her she made me feel good.

Being in love with Catherine is a different feeling than I'd ever had before. In the first months I couldn't concentrate on my work, and what was worse, I didn't care. I don't think Steve could ever understand that kind of feeling. I just wanted to abandon things...plans...and be with her. That's not the kind of person Steve sees in me. And it's been a long time since I've shown that side to Catherine. I've had to...restrain. All this contradiction is exhausting. I wanted to leave, to go home to her, but Steve was talking.

"...if you're not happy," he was saying. I hadn't heard the beginning.

"If I'm not happy..." I repeated. "I'm happy now," I said. And I thought about that. "I am happy and I love Catherine. Then why am I discussing negative things about her?"

Steve did not push and I began to work it out. "It's the future. I keep coming back to that, whenever I get this lousy feeling. It's the future! I cannot," and something began to happen to me. I felt my eyes filling with tears. "I cannot live just for the present."

"That's the *in* thing to do," Steve said.

"For me it's not enough." I felt more tears forming. I sniffed to pull them back but it was a wasted gesture. I wiped my eyes. "The future is important to me. I've got to admit that, to act on it. And the way other people see me, that's important to me. I've got to be honest with myself."

"And Catherine?"

"She's...she's different." I shook my head and wiped my cheeks. "She's just *too* different. It won't work. It's not working. I can't go on torturing myself. I've got to leave."

But I didn't. I lived with Catherine for months after that decision. I couldn't bring myself to leave her. I wanted to be with her, though we were not as happy together as we had been.

I was sure she was aware of the change in me. When she asked me what was wrong, why I was cool, I couldn't tell her I was leaving. There were times when we were joyful together, and other times when we dragged around, silently going through the motions of living, as two relatives involved in the funeral of a loved one. Our love affair had suffered a drawn-out death, without the dignity of a decent burial.

When we had our last argument and I left, I played out the role I had rehearsed in my mind many times. I held her in my arms to feel the last transference of what she would have called the presence of herself into my own self. I clung to her. I transferred the passion of my body and my longing I would have for her from my lips to hers, and then I forced myself away, avoiding her eyes that tried to hold me. I turned and walked down the stairs and I did not look back.

I drove over the freeway to Steve's.

Sandy and the baby were in the kitchen and they called out their welcome to me. I asked Steve if I could stay for a few days. Without asking any questions he simply smiled and welcomed me.

I lived through the hours of the evening and then excused myself and went into the bedroom that Sandy had prepared for me. I undressed and pulled back the covers of the bed I had never slept in before. I thought of the nights, was it only last night, when I pulled back the covers for Catherine and me. I thought of our love-making and I expected to feel an excitement and a longing, but instead I was dull. My body seemed drugged. It did not interest me. I wondered how I had ever had enough spirit to make love.

The events of our life together floated around in my mind. Had I actually done all those things? Had I sat on the beach in the cold dawn, made love like a sex-starved animal? Had I been persuaded to play in the snow almost jeopardizing my career? I felt ridiculous. Then in the next instant, when I realized that I was out of the love affair, I had a kind of purity I hadn't had in a long time like I was religiously uplifted. No longer guilty of some kind of . . . cheating myself? I couldn't define it, but I knew I would not be lying to myself anymore about who I really was and that was good.

For hours I looked at the ceiling and went over the details of my life with Catherine. It was as though I were looking at someone else. The person I tried to become repulsed me now. He was a fool. That other person, and Catherine too, had tried to break the backbone of my personality, but they had not succeeded.

It was strange. I couldn't hold on to that good feeling. My thoughts and my body were in a turmoil. It was a struggle. One minute I loved Catherine and longed for her so that I thought I would dress and return to her. The next minute I detested her because I felt foolish about the things I had done. What finally helped to settle my mind was my decision to see Father Abrams on Saturday afternoon. I had not been to confession for over a year. On Sunday, then, I would be eligible for Holy Communion and that made me feel good too.

I didn't know what time it was when I heard the phone ring. I know the apartment had been quiet for hours so it must have been about one or two o'clock in the morning. The door to my room opened and Sandy in her bathrobe stood outlined in the hall's light.

"It's for you, Kevin. The phone. I ran for it when it rang. Thank goodness it didn't wake Tommy." She left the door ajar and padded back to her bedroom.

I put on my shorts and went out into the hall and finally found the dangling receiver hanging from the wall box by the kitchen sink. I knew it would be Catherine. But at this distance I could be strong.

"Hello," I barely said.

"Kevin?"

"Yes."

"Kevin." She had been crying. "Kevin ...I've been doing a lot of thinking."

"I know. Me too."

"Kevin. I think I've finally figured out why you had to leave. It's because you want more than anything else to get married? Am I right? Did you leave because of that? Kevin? I know you told me how important it was to get married, but I never knew it meant *this* much. I didn't know you would leave."

I didn't say anything.

"Kevin. If you still want to get married ... it's okay ... I'll marry you ... Kevin?"

I couldn't seem to find what I should say. I'd *made* my decision.

"Kevin. I love you. Let's not lose our love. There's nothing more important."

"Cath," I tried. "I love you too. You know that, but...it's no good...it won't work."

"But..."

"There are too many things...too many differences."

"But if we love each other we can *make* it work. We can *change*. Look! I'm changing one of *my* differences right now. ... Remember how I always said I didn't want to get married. Well, I've just said I'd get married. And," I heard her talking very fast as if she were afraid that I might hang up. "If there are other things, well... I can change those things too."

"Yes. I know you can, Cath. *You* can change. But *I* can't. I'm sorry. I have to do this. I know I have to do this. Please understand, Cath. I know it will hurt both of us. But it's best."

"How can it be best, to break up when we *love* each other?" I could hear how hard she was trying not to cry.

"Because," I tried to explain, "the man who loves you is...he's just not *me*."

"I don't understand." She gave in to

her crying. Her sobs wrenched my heart, but I was firm.

"I know, Cath. It took me a long time to understand. I'm going to say goodbye now. I'm going to hang up. It's best...." I was trying to ignore my own tears until I could hang up. "I'm going to hang up now...Cath? Goodbye? Goodbye," I said to her...and to the man who loved her.

Chapter 6

"Sister"

I decided to confront my father in his own territory. I'd get my courage up, take time off from work, go to his house and try to talk with him. Maybe *I* could convince him that Cathy needed his help. When I telephoned her yesterday to help her get over the shock of Kevin's leaving she was filled with bitterness about a phone conversation she'd just had with Dad.

"He's so cold," she told me. "Impersonal. I'm his daughter and you'd think I was...a casual client or something."

"And that surprised you?" I asked her.

"I wanted him to help me understand something...about myself. It's the only time I've ever asked him to talk to me. Really talk to me. To help me."

"Talk to you about Kevin?"

"No. Well, yes, indirectly about Kevin. More about what the problem was between Dad and me. Why we could never talk. I'm beginning to think now there must be some connection between what *that* was and...me and...men."

I didn't know what to say. This was not the phone conversation I had anticipated.

"He always hurts me," she said.

"I know. Me too."

"Hurts *you*?"

"Yes."

"I never saw him like that with you. I thought it was only with me. He seemed okay with *you*...."

"That's because you weren't inside *my* skin," I told her. "I used to see how nice he was to other kids. When he'd pick up Aunt Karen's little girl, I'd watch him and wish he would do that with me. I don't know." I explored my memory. "I used to think he couldn't be affectionate with me because somehow I must have disappointed him. I just couldn't ever seem to please him. He always told me how to do things, after I'd already done them — wrong. I couldn't do things right. I don't know what his problem was with us."

"Whatever *his* problem, it's *our* problem now."

After that phone conversation my plan of action began. I knew when I went to his house that Betty would answer the door and then disappear and Dad and I would have privacy. So I chose a time in the late morning when I would be sure he was out of bed and probably still sober.

"He's in the den," Betty said, nodding down the hall and walking away. Dad peered at me over his glasses, lowered his book.

"Hi Honey-bun," he said. His pipe slid from his mouth onto his book. The room was dark. He sat spotlighted by the lamp from his desk. I wanted to open the drapes and let in the warm sunshine, but I knew he liked rooms that were half dark.

"What brings you here?" By the way he ran his words together I wondered how many drinks he had had. Two, I was on safe ground. Three, I could still probably get him to listen to me. Four, it would be hopeless.

"I just thought we could visit awhile." I was nervous. I was always like a trembling stranger in my father's presence. Where was that courage I had last night? "I wanted to talk to you," I said.

"Must be an epidemic. Your sister had the same problem yesterday."

"I wondered if we could..." I started and then I quit. I forced myself to start again. "Cathy needs you, Dad," I said quickly. That was not what I had meant to say, not the way I had rehearsed it.

"Needs me? She was all right last time I talked to her. What do you mean, 'needs me'? What's wrong with her?" He squinted at me, trying to focus on my face in the dark room.

"Dad... Cathy..." I stammered. Why was it when I talked to my father I felt I was auditioning to be his daughter? "Dad, could you... not be so distant with Cathy?"

He put his book on the desk. "What is it with you women?"

"How about going down to see her?" My words surprised me. Suggesting that he go to see Cathy was to be at the *end* of what I had planned to say.

"She's lived down south for five years." My words rushed out on their own. "It's only an hour's plane ride. When you go down to Los Angeles to see your friends you tell her about doing that. But Dad, you don't go to see *her*. How do you think that makes her feel?" I hadn't wanted to scold.

He stirred uncomfortably in his leather chair. "She's up here three or four times a year, why should I go down there to see her? I visit with her here," he said.

"You don't really visit, Dad. She can't come to your house here because Betty hates her. And you can't visit her at Mom's. So a couple of times a year she meets with you in restaurants."

"What's wrong with that?"

"All you've ever done with Cathy in the last five years is eat in restaurants." I had not thought much about this before. Now it seemed significant. "Your entire relationship with Cathy is reduced to polite conversation over shrimp cocktails and roast beef."

"Honey-bun," he said, beginning to be irritated. "I see you're still taking on other people's problems. Let Cathy speak for herself. You're too sensitive when other people need help."

There I was again, stopped in my tracks by, "You're too sensitive." Did my parents think telling me that would make me *in*sensitive?

Whenever Cathy or someone I loved were hurt, somehow I felt guilty of their injury and I had to try to help. If I didn't help Cathy now when I knew she was heart-sick about Kevin, I would feel that I was letting her drown. That was the way I had felt years ago about my kitten, when she had been hurt and I had not been able to help her. Not that she drowned. She had been run over by a car in front of our house.

I was a little girl then, but I always believed that I should have been able to save her. It happened on a day when Mom and Cathy had gone shopping. Dad was in the house, and I was playing on our front lawn. I saw Fluff wander out to the street and I called to her because I heard a car coming, but I didn't call loud enough. I screamed her name just before the car hit her. The driver unconcerned or unknowing, continued on down the road and disappeared from sight.

I dashed into the house screaming, "Daddy, come quick. Fluff's been hit."

He saw what had happened, ordered me to stay in the house and ran out to the road. I watched him from the front-room window. He looked down at Fluff and then went into our garage, coming out immediately with a box in his hand. I ran out of the house, reaching Fluff just as my father scooped her up in the cardboard box.

"I'll bury her, Honey-bun," he said quickly.

"*Bury* her! She's not *dead*," I yelled at him. "I saw her move! Let me see Fluff."

But he held the box up above my four-year-old head. I thought I heard Fluff thumping her legs against the box. "Let me *see* her," I pleaded.

"She's dead, Anne. You go in the house. I'll find something to wrap her in. I'll call you. You can help me bury her."

I screamed at him. "Daddy...please ...Fluff's alive! Let me see her. Let me..." I grabbed upward for the box, but he jerked my hand away. I had made him angry.

"Anne, go in the house and wait in your room." His stern voice told me to obey. "Fluff is dead," he repeated. "In a little while I'll come and get you."

But she wasn't dead. I knew that. I could have held her. I believed I could have made her well. Begrudgingly I went into the house, but not to my room. Instead I went to the kitchen door and peeked out into the garage. I heard the tools being moved around and then I saw my father pick up a hammer. He turned in my direction but didn't see me. I shut the door noiselessly.

I wanted to run out and ask him why he needed the hammer, but I couldn't. There was something in my father's nature that prevented me from pressing

177

in on him. I was helpless and filled with guilt.

Maybe my needing to help others was a way of getting rid of that guilt about not helping Fluff. Helping people made me feel good. And people helped me too. Cathy and I, we telephoned each other when we needed to. We had a hot-line ready for action. Like sometimes when all the pressures of keeping a house and having a job would get me down. I'd send my frustration five hundred miles down through the telephone lines to Cathy.

"Hal comes home from work, picks up the babies and plays with them. He's really sweet with them."

"So what's the bitch?"

"Well, he helps out maybe for an hour, sometimes even cooks the whole dinner, but then he flops in front of the TV and goes to sleep. Sometimes I wonder about life. It's housework and babies on one side, my job on the other side. It's like I'm on a tightrope."

"I can hear what you mean. I can see you up on that rope, leaning from one side and then to the other."

"It's hard, Cathy. Don't do that, Suzie," I yelled at my two-year-old climbing on to the open door of the dishwasher.

"Sometimes I think it might be easier to just fall off."

"Fall off? Hey, Anne. What do you mean?"

"Don't worry. I don't mean, 'fall off,' as in suicide if that's what you think I mean. That's not me. Especially not with two babies."

"Anne!"

"Cathy, don't jump to conclusions. Hey," I laughed, "I just realized that's what suicide is."

"Anne," she shouted over the phone.

"*Don't worry*," I shouted back a laugh in my voice. "Hang on a minute. Sally's bottle rolled away from her. I'll be right back." I dashed over to the play pen and back to the phone. "There now, where was I?"

"The tightrope."

"Oh, yeah. I don't think about that when I say about falling off the tightrope. Don't think about suicide I mean. I think it would be just easier to fall off and do the housewife bit full time."

"Could you?"

"I could, but I'd hate it. Full time, that is. It would sure make Hal happier though."

"But would *you* be happy?"

"You know I wouldn't. Suzie," I coaxed my little girl, "take this graham cracker to your little sister, okay? Here. She doesn't seem to want her bottle," I explained to Cathy. "But she's still crying."

"That tightrope bit," Cathy said, "that's kind of what I get sometimes."

"You? You're not married. How could you...you don't have problems about..."

"Don't I? You married women don't have an exclusive, you know."

"What do you mean? Suzie, don't *eat* the cracker. Give it to Sally. Here. Come get another one for yourself."

"Single women walk a tightrope too. There's a difference in the choices, that's all."

"Yeah, I guess so," though it seemed that her life was a single straight shot and mine was all curved and confusing. I reached into the refrigerator, stretching the phone cord as far as it would go. The jar of Gerber's chicken baby food was just within my reach. I took it out, slipped it into the microwave and pushed the touch-tone buttons, listening to Cathy.

"When Hal became an engineer," she was explaining to me, "he didn't have to decide if he was going to have kids and a

180

career. And on week-ends he doesn't have to make a choice between taking care of the kids, or working overtime to get his promotions."

I pushed the 'Start' button on the microwave, set for three minutes, agreeing with her. She continued. "And Allen, when he passes the state bar, he doesn't have to make a choice between his career and his love life because he knows Alicia will go where he goes. But me? If I get a job in San Francisco after *I* pass the bar, Kevin wouldn't leave his job in Los Angeles to be with me. It doesn't work that way. The decisions are women's. It's a women's tightrope."

"Well, some men..."

She knew what I was going to say and she cut me off. "Very few men are walking a tightrope. All that stuff about 'househusbands,' all those exceptions are as common as headlines that read, 'Man Bites Dog.'"

"Whew," I said. "I call you up because I'm discouraged and it sounds like you are too. I didn't help *you* any."

"I don't know. It *is* discouraging."

"Cathy, are you okay?"

"I'm okay. But it was you we were talking about to begin with. How's your job? Do the people there like you?"

"Of course. Wait a minute..." I was gone from the phone about two seconds. "Sally's getting hungry. I'll just hold her in my arms. We can talk a minute more this way. In a second she's going to really start bellowing. But why do you ask about the people on my job?"

"I have an idea." She was her cheerful self again. "Why don't you invite some of them over to your house. Have a party."

"What's that got to do with diapers."

"Nothing," she laughed.

"You're crazy," I laughed.

"Sometimes we need to be crazy. Like we used to be when we were kids. I don't see any escape for you from those diapers for a couple of years. So...make some fun for yourself. Like I said...have a party."

"Hal wouldn't agree. He's been real glum lately."

"Don't ask Hal, dummy. Arrange the party and then invite him. You guys need to have more fun in your life." I agreed with that.

The party was fun. Hal even said so. Of course I didn't tell him the party was Cathy's idea. She had told me not to. She suspected Hal's opinion of her.

"He doesn't *dis*like you, Cathy. It's . . ."

"Yes?"

"It bothers him that you're not married. And every year you seem to have a different boyfriend. He . . ."

"Don't be reluctant. *Say* it!"

"He feels you use men and then . . . dump them."

"Hmmmm."

I knew I had hurt her but I hadn't meant to.

"And do you feel that way, too, Anne?"

"No. Of course not. I'm glad you didn't marry any of those others. I liked them at the time you were going with them, but I could understand why you didn't want to marry them."

"But Hal thinks I'm just free and loose with men?"

"Not like that. Anyway, *I* think you have a good life. *You* don't have to hire babysitters if you want to get out of your house. You can go where you want to. In spite of the way I complain I wouldn't trade my life if I could, but still I can see that *you* have a good life."

I remember how we used to dream about how our lives would be. That was when we were in high school. I'd tell Cathy how in my whole life I was only going to have one boyfriend and he was going to love me all my life.

"We'll live here in Burlingame. He'll work in town, come home at night and kiss me every time before he walks in the door. And he'll tell me all the time how much he loves me."

"You want to live here all your life?"

"Sure. I'm going to stay here if I can. I like it here. My friends are here. Mom and Dad and old Scamper pooch. Why would I want to leave?"

"To see what's out in the world. I sure don't want to stay here," Cathy said. "Staying here would be putting an end to my life. When *I* graduate from high school I'm going to *start* my life."

I really believe that getting married would give Cathy the security that I have. When she found Kevin, I thought he would be the one she would marry. I could see that she really loved him. But now that was over.

Hal's referring to her as "that woman libber," irritates me. His folks make it difficult too. They see her as some kind of social misfit. I'm sure they'd forgive her for not being married if they thought she'd never been asked. Then they could feel sorry for her. But they know at least two boyfriends who wanted to marry her.

"Not respecting established custom," was the way Hal's father talked about Cathy.

"Cathy ever going to get married?" Hal's mother asked me out-of-the-blue.

"I don't know," I answered, feeling guilty.

Friends and acquaintances who knew Cathy and me when we were growing up would ask about Cathy, especially after I got married.

"And Cathy?" they'd ask, expectantly.

"She's going to law school in Los Angeles."

"Oh? I thought she was going to be a teacher?"

"Yes, well...she changed."

She can do that—change careers from teaching to law. Change jobs while she's in law school. Change boyfriends. I could never do that. I want to count on people doing what they say they're going to do. That goes back as far as the fifth grade. I can still remember my panic when Mom was going to change what she had said.

I was only ten years old and I had admired my friend's older sister because she shaved her legs. I thought that was being very grown up.

I asked my mother if I could shave *my* legs and she off-hand told me not to. "You wait a few years. You're too young to handle a razor."

That was the only time I can remember that I outright disobeyed her. I took my allowance and went to Woolworth's where I bought myself a razor. I locked myself in the bathroom and ran the sharp edge up my leg, cutting myself several times. I wiped the blood on one of Mom's good towels and then wrapped the razor in the towel and tucked it back in the corner of the bathroom linen closet.

Some days later my mother confronted me with my hidden goods. I was ashamed and admitted everything. She said she'd have to punish me, not for buying the razor so much as for disobeying her.

"You can't stay overnight with Sharon on Saturday," she announced.

Though I cried with disappointment I knew that my mother was right. But when I was cleaning and dusting my room that Saturday, Mom came in and said she'd changed her mind.

"Most of the time, Anne, you're such a good girl. I never have to tell you to clean your room, or practice the piano, or do your homework. So I'm going to skip the punishment for buying that razor. Maybe it wasn't all that important after all. Call up Sharon and tell her you can spend the night with her after all. Okay?"

"No," I cried out at her. "Don't *do* that!"

Mom was shocked.

"Please," I begged, squeezing the dust cloth in my hands. "Don't change your mind."

"I don't understand. I thought you wanted to go."

"Mom, I shouldn't have bought that razor, not after you told me not to. *Don't* let me go to Sharon's."

Mom was motionless, unspeaking for the next minute or two. Then she said, "Anne, it doesn't matter. Don't you see, honey? If *I* want to withdraw the punishment, then, it's, well, you're forgiven."

"No," I cried at her again. "Don't *do* that! Don't forgive me!"

"Oh. I think I see." I watched her studying what I had asked. "I think I understand," she said. "Yes. Don't go to Sharon's."

That was a long time ago, but I remember how concerned I was. If Mom had changed her mind about that I might still feel guilty about disobeying her. I don't know why things like that bothered me when they didn't bother Cathy. She didn't care whether other people changed their plans...except, now, with Kevin. I was sure that *his* change of heart must be hard for her.

When I finally got through to her yesterday I was going to talk to her and try to help her about Kevin's leaving, but that was when we started talking about Dad and why I had decided to go talk with him. But he had deflected my direction by bringing up my sensitivity. He told me not to be so concerned about Cathy.

"Don't worry about her. She's all right. She's... Don't take on..." He ran out of what he was going to say. I *had* a slight hope of getting somewhere, but he had turned the subject off, centering it back on my weakness. That upset me.

When he maneuvered like that I could see he kept things from getting close to him. I could see, even half-drunk, how expertly he would keep me from doing what I had come to do. He had no intention of letting me get any closer. That talk about the restaurants must have hit home. I was frustrated. I couldn't get through to him and that meant I couldn't help Cathy after all. It was the same frustration I had felt with him when Fluff died.

"Why did you kill my kitten?" I asked.

"Your *what*?" He squinted at me.

"My kitten. Fluff. With the hammer. You killed her with that hammer, didn't you?"

I had never said that, not even to myself. "All these years," I said, "I've felt guilty about Fluff. I thought that I had killed her because I didn't help her. But you wouldn't *let* me help her, just like you won't let me help Cathy now." I couldn't stop. "But *I* didn't kill Fluff. *You* did, didn't you?"

"Oh my God! That was over twenty years ago. What the Hell are you..."

"I need to know, Dad. *You* killed my kitten?"

"What the Hell's going on here?" He slammed his book shut and it fell to the floor. He was angry but I was no longer afraid of him. "You come in here, dammit Anne," he shouted at me, "and start talking about, what was it? Weren't we talking about Cathy?"

189

He reached for his pipe and began banging it upside down on the ashtray. Nothing came out of the pipe but he continued banging it.

"Do you remember Fluff, Dad?"

"Of course I remember Fluff! I remember every Goddamned thing in my life! Sometimes," he rose from his chair, stumbled. He leaned on his desk, leering at me. I don't know why he didn't scare me.

"Sometimes," he told me, "I wish I could tear my brain out of my head so I *wouldn't* remember things."

"I've never known for sure about Fluff, Dad. Why you killed her. I always felt guilty because I knew she was alive and I didn't help her. Felt *I* was responsible. I need to know what happened."

He pointed his pipe stem at me.

"There's nothing for you to know, dammit Anne."

"It's a scene from my childhood." I was relentless. "It haunts me."

"Let it go, Anne. Let those childhood pictures fade away for Christ's sake! Take it from me. Let it go! Try to forget it!"

"But I need to know. Can't you see that?"

"*Yes!*" he shouted. "*Yes*, I killed that

damn cat." He looked away from me. "You think that was any picnic? Smash in a kitten's head? And you wanted to see it. I scraped her off the road. She was all broken up. You think I can get *that* scene out of my brain. No. I haven't forgotten that picture or any other miserable picture."

He leaned his head down on the desk and for a minute I thought he was going to cry. Instead he slid open the file drawer of the desk and lifted out a bottle of brandy. He shoved the drawer shut with his foot and uncorked the half-empty bottle with his teeth, spitting the cork onto the carpet.

"Let me tell you something, Honeybun." He took a gulp from the bottle. "If you take those childhood pictures seriously they'll *consume* you."

He drank from the bottle again and though he was looking at me I could see that his eyes weren't seeing me. He walked around his desk and flopped down in his chair again, resting the bottle on his knee.

"It's not your childhood that's important," he said, looking away from me. "Childhood...that's past."

He mumbled some things I couldn't

191

catch. He wasn't talking to me. Somehow he had slipped from my childhood to his, leaving me out, retreating to his inaccessible privacy.

"If things disappoint you," he murmured to himself, "kids should forget...all those things...mothers who look like witches...and fathers...couldn't ever do anything right for him..."

He was still mumbling when I left. He half waved at me. I was leaving him in some memories I didn't know about. I knew his misery had a lot to do with his drinking but long ago I had convinced myself that was one thing I couldn't do anything about.

I had not succeeded in helping Cathy, but for the first time I had stood up to my father, and for some reason I felt relieved. Maybe it had to do with finally learning about Fluff. I felt that I had been freed from something that had a hold on me.

Chapter 7

"Mother"

I thought I would put it in a box and bury it when it was born. I would put it in a cigar box, the kind my father picked up at the corner candy store where he and I walked after dinner on Sunday afternoons. There he would buy his once-a-week treat, a medium thick Van Dyke cigar, and if the candy-store man had an empty cigar box he would give it to me. Then as we walked back home, my father would puff on his cigar, and I would lick the vanilla ice cream cone he had bought for me, trying to make it last the full four blocks.

Those Sunday walks were a special thing for us, the quiet bridge between the end of one week and the beginning of the next. My father would tell me the names of plants we saw along the way, or we'd talk about people we knew, or I'd tell him about things I had learned in school that week. I remember a Sunday-afternoon-feeling that everything was all right. And if I'd been given a cigar box, I would feel especially good.

Back home I would either give the box to my brother, Alec, to put nails in, or I'd keep it as a chest for some buttons or other treasures. We had several of those small, light balsam-wood boxes around the house. I thought of them when I learned that babies came from the kind of things we kids did when we played with our neighborhood friends. I decided to bury the baby growing in my stomach in one of those boxes.

I don't know why I assumed the baby would be born dead, or why I thought it would be small enough to fit in a cigar box. Or why I believed it might be born at anytime during the seven or eight years I worried about it, even though our games ended when I was eight years old. I did not then possess the worldly knowledge that would have told me nine and ten-year-old boys couldn't get a seven or eight-year-old girl pregnant. What my father had told me was that the play I had innocently participated in would result in my having a baby some time later. I decided that when the baby appeared I would put it in a cigar box and bury it in our large backyard where no one would ever find my terrible secret.

Of course nobody must ever know my shame, and especially not my father. Ever since he had told me where babies come from, I realized I had committed a crime that would have disappointed him greatly if he knew. He would be horrified, I was sure, if he knew he had such a bad daughter. My child's logic reasoned that my crime had been committed against him. I would have to maintain my frightening guilt all by myself.

I couldn't say to him, "Daddy, when you were at work, and when I came home from school before the babysitter got here, sometimes Alec, and I, and his friends took off our clothes in our house. Sometimes the babysitter found us and laughed at us and went and got her brother to come and join in the fun. The boys laid on top of me and moved funny and they tickled my sides to make me laugh. Daddy, I didn't know until you had that talk with me that playing like that was bad, unless I was old and married. And I didn't know it would make me have a baby. Would you help me when the baby gets born?" I would rather have died first than say anything like that to my father. I would take my chances with the cigar box.

For years at night I would lie awake in bed worrying and wondering when the baby would come. I worried, too, about becoming dumb. My father had said that people became feeble-minded or dumb when they "played with themselves." What I had done was probably worse than that. So I tested myself every night as I fell asleep to make sure I wasn't getting dumb. I added one plus one equals two plus two equals four plus four equals eight plus eight equal sixteen plus sixteen equals thirty-two and so on, until I was reassured that I had not gotten dumb, and then I fell asleep with relief.

I had learned all about babies from my father the day after my eighth birthday. "I hope you'll be pure," he had said, putting his hand on my head. He had just finished explaining that he was turning over the responsibility for housekeeping to me.

"Babysitters are a waste of money," he said, "and money is very short these days. I'm sure the three of us can do the work ourselves if we all do our share.

You're old enough now, Lisa. You're a big girl, and I'm proud of you."

Then, maybe because of the seriousness of the conversation he went on to talk about something else that was serious, what he called "the facts of life." I listened in growing astonishment. By the time he had said, "I hope you'll be pure," he had unknowingly doomed me to years of shame and guilt, because "pure," as he explained it, meant not having sex until I was married. From what he had told me, I knew I had already had sex. I could never be "pure" again. I had failed him before I was eight years old. He could not be proud of me if he had known.

Although I couldn't get back that purity, I made an immediate promise to myself that I would not play that game again, so that at least I could keep myself from getting any worse. Anyway, that game was no longer a game. It was now spoiled for me.

Though I kept expecting it for years, I had no baby. I kept my vow for over a decade, but I always felt there was a lie between my father and me. Because he assumed I was something I was not, I was cheating him of the truth. I felt that I would forever owe him something I could never pay.

Even by the time I was graduating from high school, I had a reputation as a prude because I wouldn't let any boy touch me.

"What's the point of taking Lisa on a date?" one boy told my best girl friend. "As soon as you take her home, she jumps out of the car and goes in her house."

When my friends talked in hushed tones about their sexual explorations, I was not interested. After all, I had sworn off sex at the age of eight.

My fear that my father would learn about my shameful act continued to haunt me, even when I was twenty and in love with Bob. We were in bed in a friend's apartment when an earthquake rocked the building where we were sleeping. We both awoke, hanging on to each other until the earth quit rumbling. But my panic was not from fear of the earthquake as much as it was from the fear caused by the vision I had of my father watching my dead body being dug out of the rubble where he would see that I had been in bed naked with Bob. When the earth quit shaking, I lay in Bob's arms, humiliated by my shame.

Years later, when my eight-year-old Catherine began crying, as I tucked her in bed one night, telling me she had "done something very bad," all my emotional antennae were alerted, making direct contact with my old shame. I reached for her thin shoulders, and brought her body next to me.

Holding her close I wondered about the nature of shame. In my childhood shame, because I let my father assume my "purity," I felt unworthy of his love. If he had been evil, and I had known it, would my own sin have caused me such shame? I didn't think so, because in that case he would not have been above me. It seemed to me, the great lie that parents unconsciously perpetuate with their children, until found out, is that parents are perfect.

How that must magnify a child's own imperfections! Infants grow, stumble, break things, spill food, urinate at the wrong time, and cry out loud when they're hurt, in a world of adults who seem to do everything right. "I am bad and you are good," the child feels—Catherine with me—me with my father. On this night it would be important for my child to know that I was as fallible as she.

After she had cried for awhile I urged her to tell me about it. "But only if you want to."

"I *have* to tell you, Mom," she cried. "I was very bad."

I thought she might be magnifying the problem, whatever it was, but if Catherine felt bad about it then she needed help in getting over it. I didn't want her to keep any burden of guilt hidden inside of *her*. Between my father and me, each of us hiding a secret from the other, we'd carried enough guilt for one family.

"Anne and I and Marie," Catherine sobbed, "when you let us out to play at Jefferson School, while you visited with Marie's mom, we..." She choked up.

I stroked her hair, soothing her, waiting for the bad feelings to flow out.

"We took some of Marie's chalk from her house and went to the school. Then we...wrote...a dirty word all over the building."

With that she wept convulsively, her shoulders shaking. I patted her and hugged her, wondering how to help her forgive herself. She had made me her judge. What was the delicate balance, I

200

wondered, not between crime and punishment, but between punishment and restoration of self? How could I help her find it?

"What did you write?" I asked, stalling for time.

"We wrote, 'Fuck you,' all over the walls," she whispered, pulling back to see how I would react.

I stopped stroking.

"What does that mean?" I asked.

"Don't *you* know, Mom?"

"Yes. But I want to know what *you* think it means." I dried her cheeks with the edge of her bed sheet.

"I don't know. I asked Marie and she wouldn't *tell* me."

"Then why did you think it was a dirty word? Maybe it's *not*."

"Marie said it was a *terrible* word. She said it was the worst word in the whole world, and that if we got caught we would have to...go to jail!" She cried again folding up in my arms.

Catherine didn't know the meaning of the words she had chalked on the side of the school. But, I worried, she could continue to feel guilty about her "sin," unless I could give her some way to make amends or wipe it out. I wanted to help her, but I wasn't sure how. If I could talk to Bob...but he never seemed to want to get involved.

"I think that tomorrow, if you take a rag," I suggested, "and wipe the words off the building."

"Oh, *no*, Mom!" she cried. "Someone will see me."

"They may." I wondered about that too. "If anyone does, you can simply explain that you wrote those words, but decided it wasn't right to do that, so you came back to clean it up."

"I'll feel *awful* if I'm caught!"

I thought about that. Maybe I was asking for too much. "Don't you feel awful now?"

"Yes!"

"Well, you might feel awful for a long, long time if you don't erase those words." I paused. "If you do erase them, and I'll help you, you'll feel better."

"What about Anne and Marie? Don't they have to do it too?"

"Anne will go with us, but Marie is her family's problem." I sat her up and looked at her. "Think you can try?"

She was silent. Then she said quietly, hanging her head, "I'll try."

"I'll help you," I offered again.

"Thank you," she said with a weak smile.

"I'll help you because when I was little and did some wrong things, if Grandpa knew about them, he helped me. I remember one time, especially, when he helped Uncle Alec get over what *he* did."

"You mean *you* and *Uncle Alec* did bad things?"

"Sure!"

"What kind of things?"

"Oh I don't remember all the details," I lied, not wanting to change the focus of our talk. But I remembered.

Putting my head on hers, I thought of the time the policeman had come to our front door when Alec and I were young. We were so frightened we had hidden behind the door. But my father was brave. He stepped right out on the front porch in his undershirt.

I'd always thought people would get arrested if they were caught outside with their underwear showing. My father had just come home from work. He'd taken off his shirt and pulled his pants' suspenders over his undershirt. I was worried he might get arrested for that, but then Alec and I started listening to what the policeman was saying. He wasn't talking about underwear at all. He was saying something about cherries stolen from the Williams's cherry tree.

"The neighbors on the other side of the Williams's said they saw your son, Alec, stripping the tree," the policeman said. "He climbed up and took off all the cherries, tossing them down to the little kids below. The Williams have been waiting all year for those cherries."

"You're sure it was Alec?" my father asked.

"No question about it."

I stared at Alec. He looked grey, the way he looked when he was going to vomit.

Stepping backward, my father reached his big arm around the doorway and grabbed Alec by his ear. Alec yelled and stumbled out on the porch.

"Here he is officer. Take him away."

Then Alec and I both yelled. I came out of hiding to plead with my father not to send Alec to jail. I wanted him to tell the policeman that Alec was really a good boy. And besides, my brother was only ten years old.

"Well," the policeman said sternly, "stealing is a very serious crime."

"I'll never do it again!" Alec pleaded, tears running down his cheeks. "I promise—honest!"

My father said, "When Alec promises something, officer, he means it. He never goes back on a promise—I'll vouch for that."

"That the truth, son?" the policeman asked.

"Yes!" The tears were still flowing.

"It's *true!*" I put in desperately, hoping to save Alec.

"Well," the policeman frowned, "maybe we'll let it go *this* time. On one condition."

Alec wiped his cheek with his sleeve. "Sure," he whispered.

"Apologize to the Williams family."

"Oh *no!*" Alec wailed, fresh tears gushing. "Dad, do I *have* to?"

"No," my father said solemnly. "You can go to jail."

Alec wept freely. "I'll apologize."

Now these many years later, holding my daughter in my arms, I thought about the lesson my father and that policeman had taught my brother and me years ago, by their unrehearsed performance. My father had helped Alec get rid of his guilt feelings. I thought again also about the secret burden of guilt that *I* had carried for many years. I didn't want Catherine to carry any similar guilt into *her* adulthood.

I wondered how I could apply what I had learned from that experience. I wished vaguely that I could call on Bob to help Catherine learn something here, as I had learned from *my* father. I also wanted her to learn that people she looked up to were not perfect. I wanted to tell her "Don't revere me. It's not healthy." But she wouldn't understand.

Finally I said, "We *all* did bad things, Catherine."

She looked at me sideways—unbelieving. "Even Daddy?"

"Even Daddy."

She was quiet for a long time thinking about that. Then she asked, "Everybody?"

"Everybody. Everybody you see walking down the street. They *all* once did bad things. But their lives go on. Their world didn't come to an end."

"You mean it doesn't *matter* what they did?"

"Oh, it matters. But often you pay for such mistakes, and that makes things better. Then, if you're intelligent—and

206

you certainly are—you learn to forgive yourself."

"Will *you* forgive me?" Catherine asked wistfully.

"That's not what's important," I said, thinking it out slowly. "The important thing is to understand why what you did was wrong, and decide what you're going to do about it, so you won't have to carry around a lot of awful feelings about it. You don't want those feelings to pile up on you."

Then I added, "What's really important is that you learn to forgive yourself."

"Why can't *you* forgive me?"

"Because you didn't do anything against *me*. You did something against yourself. Did you think it was wrong?"

"Yes."

"Why did you tell me about it?"

"Because I felt awful, and I didn't want to go to sleep without telling you. I felt like it would be lying to you if I didn't tell you."

"Did you feel if you told me, then I could make it better?"

"Yes." She hugged me. "I knew you would."

"You feel better? You can go to sleep now?"

"Yes. I'll go erase the writing tomorrow." She thought a minute, then added, "Don't tell Daddy? Please."

"Daddy and I don't have secrets from each other. You're *our* little girl, not just *my* little girl."

"He'll *hate* me!" she moaned, pulling back. "I don't want him to know—ever!"

Old memories of my secret guilt with my father came back to me again. "If he didn't know, you might have more bad feelings for keeping a secret from him. You might feel that you *owed* him something."

"I don't know what you're talking about. I just don't want him to know, that's all." She began to cry. "I'd rather *die*! I don't want him to know I'm *bad*."

"You're not bad. You just did something wrong. I told you, *all* of us do wrong things sometimes."

"I don't care. He'll think I'm bad. He hardly ever talks to me as it is. He *never* thinks I do anything good. He won't *love* me!"

"Oh yes he will." I patted her arm. "Catherine, it's not up to you whether Daddy knows or not. It's up to me. I'll tell him and he'll understand."

Her sobs became convulsive again. I comforted her and tucked her blankets around her. Her tears gradually subsided. I kissed her, turned off her light and shut her bedroom door, leaving her alone with her fears and with her thoughts.

My heart was with her. I didn't know if I'd really helped her. I always felt all alone in trying to do the right things. But I could never tell whether I was doing well at all with the children. Nothing was ever clear-cut. I felt that maybe I had eased one problem for Catherine. But in doing so, had I created another?

When Bob came home later that night I told him about the whole thing as we were getting ready for bed. I wanted him to take some part in resolving what was a difficult problem for Catherine and me.

"She's *what*?" he asked incredulously. "Going *back* to erase the writing? You must be out of your mind, Lisa."

I stiffened. "What's wrong with that idea?"

"Well, dammit, the principal of that school catches her erasing that wall, asks her name...how do you think that will make *me* look in this town?"

"But she needs a way to make

amends...to stop feeling guilty.

"Then think of something else," he said emphatically.

"Will *you* talk to her? Maybe you could make her feel better about what she did. It's important to her, what you think."

"Yeah...well...yeah. I'll talk to her. When I get a chance." But I knew he never would. He never did.

The next morning I woke Catherine and Anne early and we drove to Jefferson School long before anyone else arrived. My girls jumped out of the car, wet rags in hand. They ran across the playground and into a shrubbed area under the classroom windows.

"In *here*, Mom," Catherine whispered urgently, holding a thorned bush aside for me to crouch under. Squatting under the shrubs I looked up to see where the windows were, but found they were obscured by the thick growth. I looked back toward the playground and realized that the branches had flopped back into place, hiding us from view.

"You wash that one, Anne," Catherine directed her sister hurriedly, "and I'll do this one here."

I was astounded. With difficulty I

could make out four or five small sized printed words on the pinkish stucco.

"*There*!" Catherine said after less than a minute. "I erased Marie's too." They both scrambled out of the shrubs, leaving me to crawl out by myself. They ran back to the car and I followed at a walk.

"Hurry up, Mom," Anne pleaded from the car. "Let's *go*!"

"Are there *more* places?" I was confused. "Was that... the only place?"

"Yes, Mom. Let's *go*! Let's get out of here before the kids start coming to school."

That was the *sin*? In my relief and amazement I dared not smile. I knew its seriousness.

Bob needn't have worried about the principal seeing the girls, or about his precious image. Maybe I should have told him. But I tried to get him to share equally in raising our girls. I knew I loved them. Though after they were born he told me, "having kids is the end of my life," words that hung heavy for me ever after.

I hoped as the girls grew, Bob would get caught up in their lives. Instead he became more and more caught up in responsibilities and in the community. The community loved him because he was generous with his time. He thrived on adulation from his colleagues, customers, secretaries, prospective employees, from the San Mateo County's P.T.A. Board, Planning Commission, and all those charitable fundraisers that he lent his time and talents to. By comparison, his responsibilities at home were a burden.

"I know this sounds psychotic," he told me one night when our girls were little, "but there are days when I'm at work and I think of you and the kids and I wish the house and all three of you would blow up."

I understood all the pressures he was under. Though I, too, was employed and had the added responsibility of the household, it was Bob who was overwhelmed.

I knew he worked hard, but I tried not to take away his share of the responsibility for decisions for our children. I was afraid, if they became *my* children alone, whatever family unity we had would be destroyed. I was convinced of that as early as Catherine's second week of life.

She'd been crying all day, and nothing I could do would stop it. When Bob came home late from work, I watched him from the window of our apartment with Catherine in my arms, as he parked his car. He made several wobbly attempts before he brought the car to the curb. Finally he opened the car door and weaved around to the sidewalk. A few minutes later I heard him come up the stairs slowly. I opened the apartment door, Catherine crying.

"Hello, darling," he said, "and how's my little Cathy?" He nuzzled his nose against her face, almost knocking me over.

"She's been crying all day," I said. "I don't know what's wrong."

"Crying? Well, let me take care of *that*. *I'll* stop her crying. Come to Daddy." He took her from me.

I worried that in his condition he might drop her, but I let him hold her because she was *his* child too. I dared not point out that he was drunk. It would lead to a fight, maybe violence. Once he'd thrown me against a plate glass window. So, our infant in his arms, I said nothing, but I watched him anxiously.

Stumbling and weaving, he carried our two-week-old baby around the room, mumbling incoherent endearments to soothe her tears. I watched him bump into furniture and catch himself from falling. I held my breath. After about half an hour of futile efforts to end Catherine's tireless crying, he quickly handed her to me, then darted into the bathroom. I heard him throwing up.

Yes, Catherine was his child too, whether he was drunk or sober. We would just have to live through the bad times to get to the good.

But when it all reached a point of diminishing returns, and there weren't any more good times together, I wondered why I continued to love him. I couldn't find any reason. My love for Bob was not something I could analyze. I simply loved him.

There had been several men it would have been smarter for me to love. Men whose parents had large landholdings or businesses. Men who are today multi-millionares, besides being nice men. But I didn't love them, and I never would have. The chemistry wasn't there.

It was there for Bob, the lover I had met when I was twenty. And that chemistry was a smoke screen for the danger signals I should have seen in our first months together.

"He drinks too much," my father said the first month we began dating. "He won't leave the bottle alone until it's empty."

I hadn't noticed.

"He's very intelligent," my father acknowledged. "And he's a smart dresser. I like to talk to him—he has a wealth of knowledge." I felt proud. "And he has a social presence you don't see often in young people nowadays."

It made me happy to hear that.

But I was concerned when he added, "On the other hand, Lisa, he's sometimes sarcastic. Sometimes mean."

I hadn't noticed. Not right away. But I hadn't really seen Bob's dark side until after about twenty-three years of marriage. One night after an argument he had grabbed me by the neck and knocked my head savagely against the kitchen wall. I had felt my life leaving my body. Yet even then the chemistry was so strong that, as he was choking me, I told myself he might as well kill me, because I didn't want to live if he wanted me dead.

I saved my life by not struggling.

When I didn't fight back, his passionate rage subsided. His hands went limp, and my survival instincts took over. I skirted around the corner from the kitchen into the dining room, then down the hall. I heard him coming after me again.

"Don't come a step closer!" I cried. "Or I'll kick you in the balls!"

I flung out my foot. He reached to protect himself, giving me a split second to dash into the study. I shoved a chair against the door, reached swiftly for the phone, and dialed our neighbors, Dan and Alice, down the lane.

"Please!" I cried. "This is Lisa—come quick!"

In two minutes I saw their car lights and heard their running feet. Dan stayed in the kitchen with Bob while Alice hurried to the study and asked me what had happened.

"He came home late again," I said weakly. "Last night he was at Jenny Birch's. She called me to tell me he was on his way home. Tonight he was late again. The kids went to the show. I usually never say anything to him about coming home late, but tonight I had a special dinner for the two of us. A celebration for his promotion. I mentioned I was disappointed that he hadn't come home. He got nasty and sarcastic. I lost my temper and yelled at him. It was the first time in our marriage that I ever yelled at him. In twenty-three years!"

"What did you yell?" Alice asked.

"I yelled, 'If it's too hard for you to come home, then don't *come* home!' He flew into a rage and choked me."

I cried with the memory, feeling the soreness where his fingers had crushed my throat.

"When I got free, I ran down the hall. He came after me with a look in his eyes I'd never seen before. His eyes were crazy. He shouted, 'You *yelled* at me, dammit! *Just like my mother!*'"

"Bob never attacked you before?"

"Never. Not like this."

Alice sat down, sighing. "Hell, Lisa, in our house it's routine."

"My God! You never said anything about it! Why?"

She lit a cigarette thoughtfully. "Who am I gonna' tell? Who'd believe anything like that about Dan? He's a big shot, remember! People look up to him in this town. Who'd believe *me*? And where would I go after I told on him? You ... you have a job. But *I* can't support myself.

Not after all these years. He never let me work, you know. Said it would reflect bad on him."

I didn't want to think about that, yet.

After awhile Alice and I went into the kitchen. Bob was noisily putting dishes into the cupboard. He looked at me.

"I suppose," he said sarcastically, "you told Alice I tried to *kill* you?"

I didn't reply.

"Lisa," Dan advised me paternally, "take my word for it. Bob is *not* having an affair with Jenny."

So Bob had told Dan that I was upset about Jenny! He was clever. He knew if he talked about Jenny, that would get everybody's mind off his attack on me. Make *me* wrong. Make *me* deserving of his wrath. But I knew the truth.

Bob had revealed it to me in the words still ringing in my ears: "You yelled at me, dammit! Just like my mother!"

Bob hadn't been choking me. It was his *mother* he was trying to kill.

I decided not to confront him with the truth. In my anguish all I wanted now was to get rid of the terrible memory. I was, after all, still my father's daughter.

Emotions controlled, trauma swept under the rug.

Nearly murdered, I did not want to fight back. What was paralyzing me? A death wish? Surprise? Fear? Love? Or the need for dignity even now, when there was no dignity? What did it matter?

All I wanted was for Dan and Alice to go back down the lane, and for Bob to take me in his arms, to tell me that he loved me, and to ask me to forgive him as he had done once fifteen years before.

That time he had been demonstrating how he had hit a sarcastic taxi driver in the mouth. All his latent anger must have rushed forth. The driver's false teeth had bounced out into the snow. Feeling sorry for the cab driver, Bob had helped him search for the teeth in the snow.

Then he had come upstairs, very drunk and upset, and to show me what he had done he accidentally hit me in the mouth, and the blood flowed down my chin. He'd cried and retreated, begging me to forgive him, which I did because I hardly noticed.

This time, also, I would gladly not have noticed. But now he was cold, distant. For two silent weeks we went about our lives, not speaking of anything and especially not of what had happened. We ignored it.

Then one night in bed we touched each other. The chemistry flowed. We caressed and began to make love. But before I could bring myself to it wholly I wanted to clear the air. I wanted to forgive him, to get what had happened that night out in the open so we could get rid of its oppressive presence. When I began to talk about it he took his hands off my body and moved to the far side of the bed.

"You deserved it," he snapped, turning from me. And then he said, "And I'd do it again."

In a little while I heard his snoring.

I *deserved* it? Deserved to be *murdered*? I believed that Bob simply couldn't face what he had done. So he had to keep *me* in the wrong.

Yet even after that, I still loved him for three more years. What does it take for the chemistry to change?

I unexpectedly returned home from work early one day and found the remains of his loving tryst with Jenny in our home. *That* was the day the chemistry that had been a part of my body and my emotion for most of my life dissolved. I said aloud to the empty house, "I am no longer in debt."

I hadn't even known that I was *in* debt.

What debt?

Living a lie, I answered. My marriage was a fraud. I would get a divorce. I would finally admit the failure of my marriage. I would hurt us all, reveal our weaknesses, our humanness. The truth that would set me free would thrust me into a fearful, terrifying unknown world. But the only other choice was a bondage to the lie. I had finally learned the lesson that had been presenting itself to me through my life. A lie—any lie—I realized, is a moral debt.

"You'll make statistics out of the kids," Bob snarled at me after I left. I shrugged.

"Mercy," he begged, days later. "I love you and our girls." I stared at him. *Now* you tell me, I might have said, but I no longer cared that much.

"Suicide," his note read two weeks later. "Life is not worth living without you." It *had* been, I could have written. Instead, I alerted his friends to help him, and I sent Bob a note, "I will not be responsible for your death."

"See how cruel she is," our friends said, flocking to console him, turning against me.

Some kind of wall protected me from his pleadings. For a year. Then that wall surprisingly disintegrated, and surgings of the old chemistry awakened me.

"Come back," I wrote. "Let's work it out."

I ran out to meet his car. Like a breathless teenager I kissed him open-mouthed. We walked hand-in-hand into our house.

"Lisa, there's something I have to tell you. The wedding's set...with Betty... Saturday, next."

"Wedding? Next Saturday? My God, a wedding...Saturday is...*our anniversary!*"

He looked out the window. "I've asked the church," he said, "to grant me an annulment so I can...Betty's Catholic...."

"Bob, what are you doing? Annul our marriage? How can a marriage that lasted twenty-six years be annulled?"

"It's just a church formality."

"Bob, what are you doing?" I asked

again. "Please," I began to implore, "if we went in for counseling..."

He paced the floor, not listening. I could feel his disappearance. My chemistry in charge, I reached out with desperate pleadings.

"I've had time to think...come home ...we had so much. More than a quarter of a century...." Why did I sound so weak, so unconvincing? He was walking toward the door. "The girls..." my voice was fading. "And we'll have grandchildren..."

"Lisa." He opened the door and turned to me. "It's out of my hands. Yesterday Betty's father bought the bedroom set."

I watched his car until it was out of sight, wondering why I had set myself up for his rejection one more time. Had I really been that unconvinced?

Now, ten years after my divorce, I sit here watching the clouds below the window of a 747 as I fly down to help my grown-up daughter recover from *her* heartbreak. My own recovery had taken time, but the worst wounds healed as the years passed. The scar tissue thickened. I managed to get on with my life as I'm sure Catherine will too.

I cling to the foolish hope that she'll fall out of love with Kevin soon, and that she won't have to live through a regression as I did. Yet I, of all people, ought to know better. I recall the exhilaration of falling in love, and the agony of falling out of love. Yet, I smile, thinking that like childbirth, most of us willingly and joyfully go on to do it again.